Chord Chemist

GW00361535

Chord Chemistry

Wise Publications
London / New York / Paris / Sydney / Copenhagen / Madrid / Tokyo

Exclusive distributors:

Music Sales Limited
8/9 Frith Street, London W1V 5TZ, England.

Music Sales Pty Limited
120 Rothschild Avenue, Rosebery, NSW 2018,
Australia.

Order No. AM942580
ISBN 0-7119-7820-4
This book © Copyright 2000 by Wise Publications.

Written and arranged by Arthur Dick and Dave Holmes.
Music processed by Digital Music Art.
Book design by Michael Bell Design.
Edited by Sorcha Armstrong.
CD programmed by John Moores.
Recorded by Kester Sims.
All Guitars by Arthur Dick.
Photography by George Taylor.

Printed in the United Kingdom by
Printwise (Haverhill) Limited, Haverhill, Suffolk.

Your Guarantee of Quality
As publishers, we strive to produce every book to
the highest commercial standards.
Particular care has been given to specifying acid-free,
neutral-sized paper made from pulps which
have not been elemental chlorine bleached.
This pulp is from farmed sustainable forests and was
produced with special regard for the environment.
Throughout, the printing and binding have been
planned to ensure a sturdy, attractive publication
which should give years of enjoyment.
If your copy fails to meet our high standards,
please inform us and we will gladly replace it.

Music Sales' complete catalogue describes
thousands of titles and is available in full colour
sections by subject, direct from Music Sales Limited.
Please state your areas of interest and send a
cheque/postal order for £1.50 for postage to:
Music Sales Limited, Newmarket Road,
Bury St. Edmunds, Suffolk IP33 3YB.

www.musicsales.com

Introduction

From Blues to Funk, Chord Chemistry will help you discover the chords you need to play your favourite songs!

What is Chord Chemistry?

We've all watched someone play and wondered - 'What's that chord? It sounds great!'. Now Chord Chemistry shows you how to create those great-sounding chords and chord sequences.

What will I learn?

Right from the start you'll find out how to spice up your basic repertoire, creating chords like **add** and **sus**. You'll also learn how to create 7ths and 9ths, and how to mix slash, root, pedal and barre chords into your sequences.

How will I know if it sounds right?

Throughout, you'll be able to listen to the accompanying CD for tips.
And that's not all! Soon you'll be playing a complete song in 3 different styles, to the accompaniment of specially-recorded professional backing tracks.

Chord Chemistry is the exciting new way to transform your basic chord skills into professional-sounding guitar parts!

 **TRACK 1**

Tuning

Use the notes supplied on Track 1 of the CD to tune your guitar, before you start playing along with the backing tracks.

The strings are played as follows (from high to low): **E B G D A E**

Listen carefully as you tune, trying to match exactly the pitch of each note.

Each track on the CD has two bars count-in.

> **TUNING**
> Use track 1 on the CD
> to tune your guitar

. The Basics

Here are five classic chords - in fact, they're probably the first chords you ever learned. They can be used to create hundreds of songs and chord sequences. Make sure that you are familiar with them as many of the chords used throughout the book are based on these five shapes.

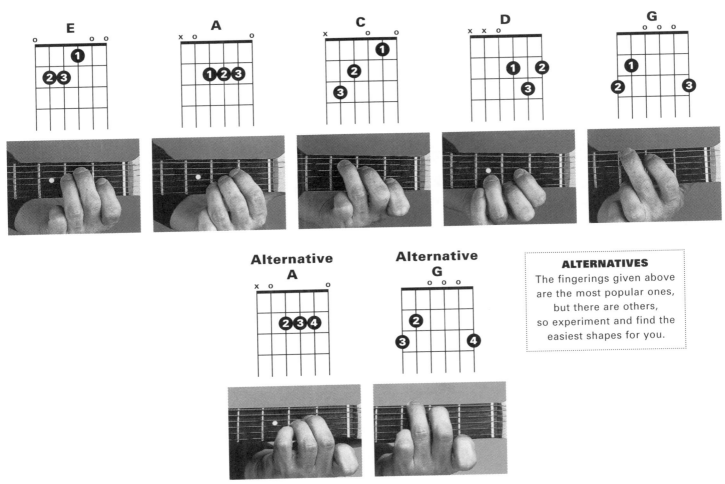

ALTERNATIVES
The fingerings given above are the most popular ones, but there are others, so experiment and find the easiest shapes for you.

Fretbox & Chord Notation Diagrams Explained

The **X** symbol means you should not play this string
The **O** symbol means 'open': no fingers should touch the string

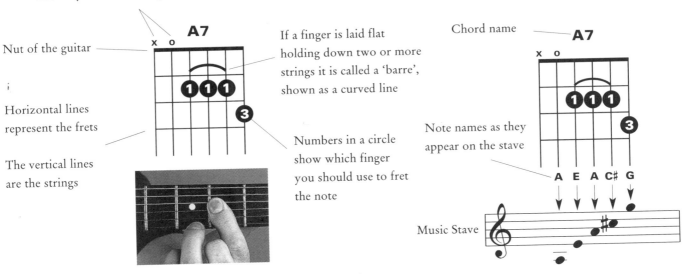

Nut of the guitar

Horizontal lines represent the frets

The vertical lines are the strings

A7

If a finger is laid flat holding down two or more strings it is called a 'barre', shown as a curved line

Numbers in a circle show which finger you should use to fret the note

Chord name — **A7**

Note names as they appear on the stave

Music Stave

A E A C# G

Throughout this book we will also use pictures to show you the correct position of your fretting hand on the guitar

'Fifth Avenue'

Now listen to the CD and try these five chords in this classic sequence. There are two versions of each example on the CD; the first is a demonstration version, so that you can hear how the track *should* sound - the second is a backing track for you to play along with.

TRACKS 2+3

TIP
Chords are arranged in the order in which they happen in the song to help you memorise the sequence.

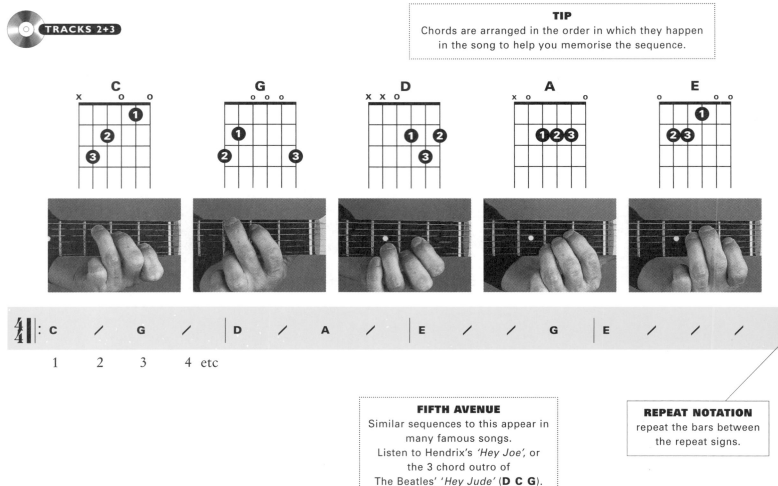

FIFTH AVENUE
Similar sequences to this appear in many famous songs.
Listen to Hendrix's *'Hey Joe'*, or the 3 chord outro of The Beatles' *'Hey Jude'* (**D C G**).

REPEAT NOTATION
repeat the bars between the repeat signs.

Chord Notation

To understand chords and how they work we need to look to the scale that relates to that particular chord. For a chord of **C**, the **C** major scale is the raw material. If it were **G** it would be **G** major, and so on.

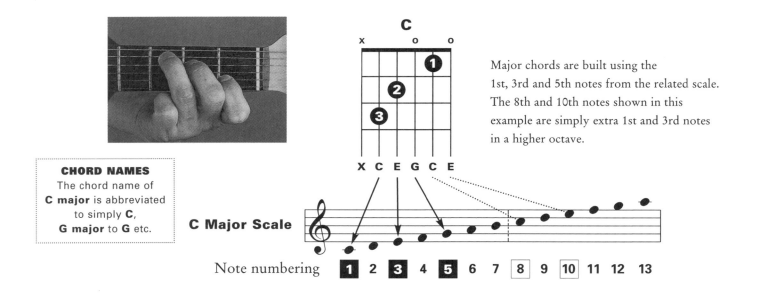

Major chords are built using the 1st, 3rd and 5th notes from the related scale. The 8th and 10th notes shown in this example are simply extra 1st and 3rd notes in a higher octave.

CHORD NAMES
The chord name of **C major** is abbreviated to simply **C**, **G major** to **G** etc.

2. Spicing Up The Open Chord

'Three Chord Trick'

Try this straightforward chord sequence - it sounds good, but with a little Chord Chemistry
we can make it sound great!

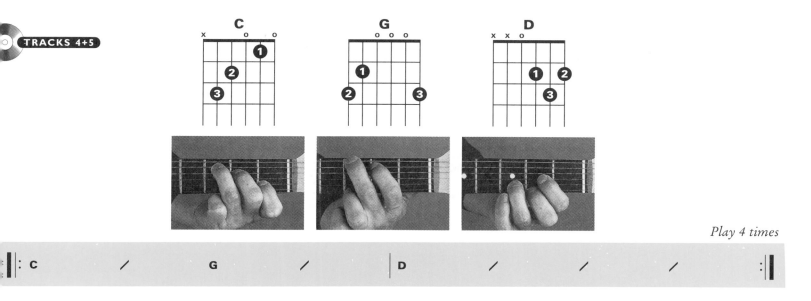

TRACKS 4+5

Play 4 times

‖: C   /   G   / | D   /   /   /   :‖

'Spice It Up'

Now check out this chord sequence - it sounds dramatically different to 'Three Chord Trick',
but it fact it's based on exactly the same chords.

TRACKS 6+7

> **THEORY TIP**
> In this example
> we have changed
> the chords in
> the sequence,
> while maintaining
> the harmonic
> movement -
> we call this
> *Chord Substitution*.

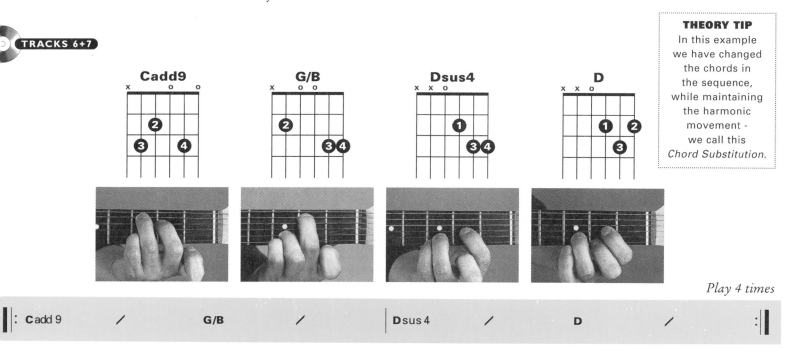

Play 4 times

‖: Cadd 9   /   G/B   / | Dsus 4   /   D   /   :‖

Sounds better, doesn't it? Remember that the chords in 'Spice It Up' are not really any
different from those in 'Three Chord Trick'. They are still essentially **C**, **G** and **D**, but have been
altered by adding notes from the scale. This is a simple, natural progression, and makes the
sequence sound more interesting.

Don't think of **Cadd9** as a chord completely different to **C**, the **add9** is only an addition to
the basic chord. The same applies to **G/B** and **Dsus4**. Most professional players incorporate this
kind of chord thinking into their songs and sequences.

What does the chord name Cadd9 mean?

The **add9** literally means add the 9th note of the scale, **D**, to the chord of **C** that you already know. You will notice that the process of 'adding' the note on the fretboard is actually one of replacement - what was a **C** on the 2nd string (1st fret) is now raised 2 frets to **D**.

TECHNICAL TIP
Because the **D** is considered an addition to the major third, the **add9** description is used rather than **add2**, however, it doesn't mean the **9th** has to be the top note of the chord.

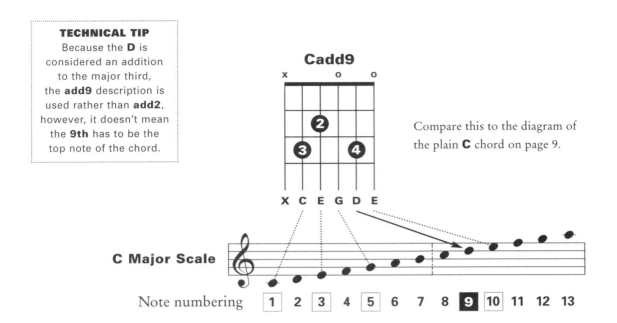

Cadd9

Compare this to the diagram of the plain **C** chord on page 9.

C Major Scale

Note numbering 1 2 3 4 5 6 7 8 9 10 11 12 13

Here are the five easiest **add9** shapes based on the open chords that you already know.

Eadd9   Aadd9   Cadd9   Dadd9   Gadd9

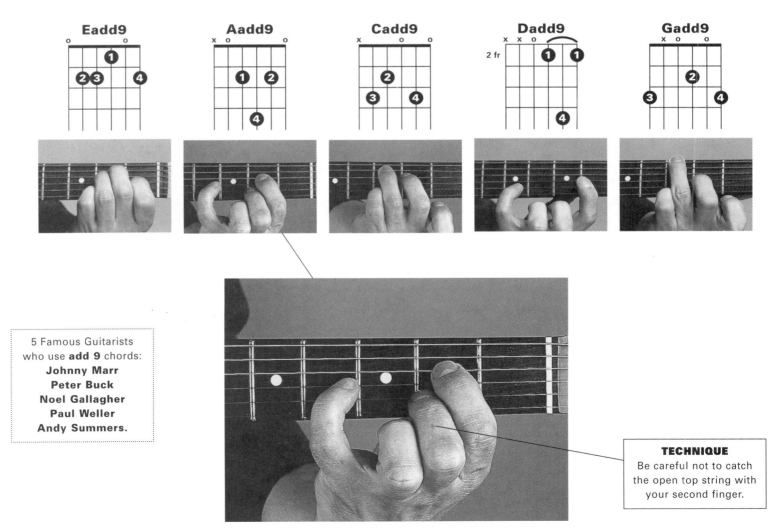

5 Famous Guitarists who use **add 9** chords:
Johnny Marr
Peter Buck
Noel Gallagher
Paul Weller
Andy Summers.

TECHNIQUE
Be careful not to catch the open top string with your second finger.

'Wide Open'

Here's a sequence that sounds great using strummed or picked chords...

The famous **Police** song *'Message In A Bottle'* has **Andy Summers** adding up all his ninths.

TRACKS 8+9

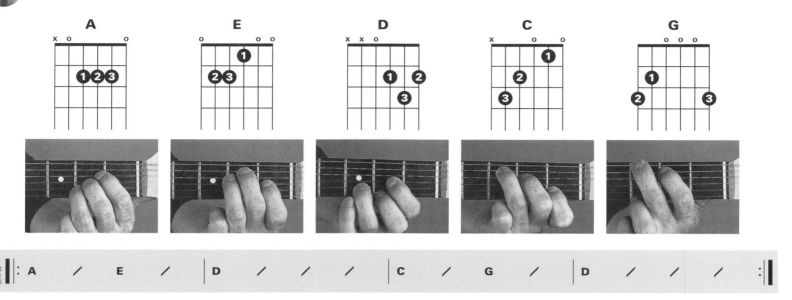

'Nine In The Morning'

But now try adding 9ths to all these chords and hear how the flavour of the piece becomes more mellow.

TRACKS 10+11

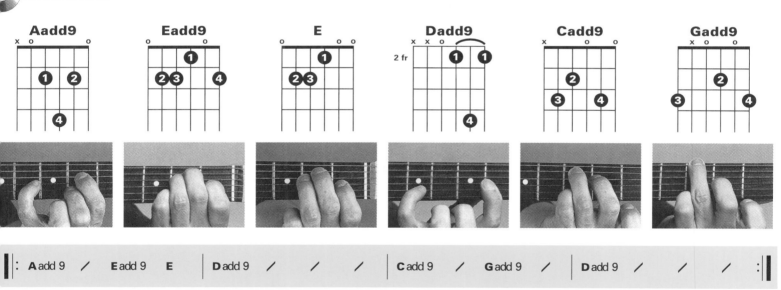

Try these alternative versions of **Cadd9** and **Eadd9**. As with all these chords, take care not to catch the open strings.

TECHNICAL TIP
CHORD VOICING
There is often more than one way to voice (make up) a chord. These are the same chords as those given above, the notes are just in a different order.

Alternative
Cadd9

Alternative
Eadd9

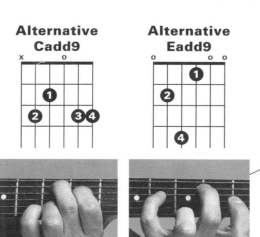

11

What other notes can I add?
Exploring the sus4

The fun doesn't stop with adding 9ths to these chords - in fact that's only the beginning. Other tones from the scale can also be added to the basic major chord shapes. Some of these tones can have a dramatic impact on the sound of the chord and the feel of the piece - check out what happens when we include the 4th degree of the scale in a **C major** chord:

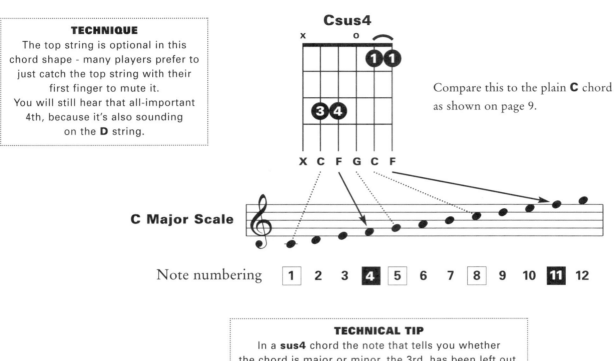

Compare this to the plain **C** chord as shown on page 9.

TECHNIQUE
The top string is optional in this chord shape - many players prefer to just catch the top string with their first finger to mute it.
You will still hear that all-important 4th, because it's also sounding on the **D** string.

Csus4

X C F G C F

C Major Scale

Note numbering 1 2 3 **4** 5 6 7 **8** 9 10 **11** 12

TECHNICAL TIP
In a **sus4** chord the note that tells you whether the chord is major or minor, the 3rd, has been left out. It's replaced by the 4th - this is called a suspension, because the 4th sounds as though it wants to fall to the 3rd.

So why is this chord not called add4?

Simple - in an **add** chord the 3rd note of the scale is also present, and the new note is added to it. In a **sus** chord the third has been omitted - that's the only difference!

Here are the five easiest **sus4** shapes based on the five open major chord shapes:

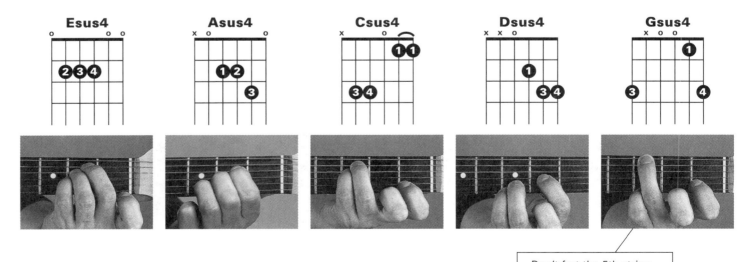

Esus4   Asus4   Csus4   Dsus4   Gsus4

Don't fret the 5th string - just allow your third finger to mute it.

'Nice & Easy'

Let's take a typical chord sequence and add some Chord Chemistry with **sus4** chords.
Listen to Track 12 and then try playing along (strumming or picking) with this simple sequence
of open chords.

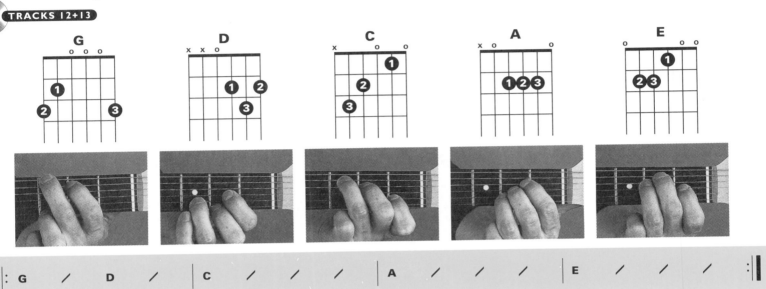

TRACKS 12+13

'Down On 4th Street'

Now check out how this sequence can be livened up with the addition of **sus4** chords in
every bar. The typically unresolved and "open" flavour of this sequence is entirely due to the
sus4s - the 4th degree of the scale in each **sus4** chord creates tension because it wants to
resolve to the 3rd.

TRACKS 14+15

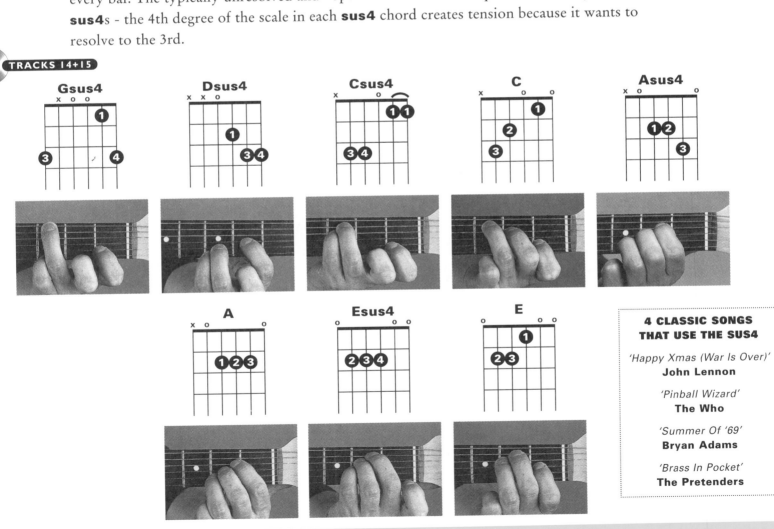

**4 CLASSIC SONGS
THAT USE THE SUS4**

'Happy Xmas (War Is Over)'
John Lennon

'Pinball Wizard'
The Who

'Summer Of '69'
Bryan Adams

'Brass In Pocket'
The Pretenders

You know sus4 – now try sus2

You've already seen how we can raise the 3rd in a chord to make a **sus4** chord. We can also lower the third to create a **sus2**:

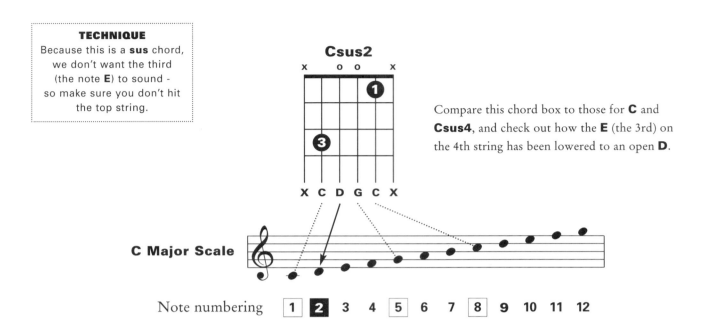

Compare this chord box to those for **C** and **Csus4**, and check out how the **E** (the 3rd) on the 4th string has been lowered to an open **D**.

2 or 9 – what's the difference?

Many budding Chord Chemists find it difficult to understand the difference between **sus2** and **add9**. Why use 2 in one chord name and 9 in the other, when the 2nd note of the scale and the 9th are the same thing?

Chord theory dictates that when a note is added it is taken from outside the original octave - hence the 9. But when a note in the original chord is altered (as in a **sus** chord) it is thought of as coming from inside the original octave - hence the **sus2**. Hence, in any **add** chord, the third degree of the scale is still present, whereas it is removed in a **sus** chord.

Here are the five easiest **sus2** chords based on the open major chords:

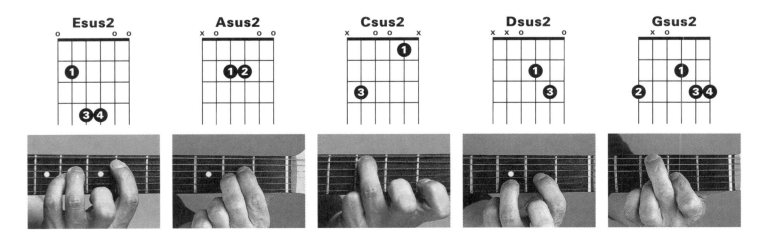

'Lucky Dip'

With **add9**, **sus2** and **sus4** chords at your disposal, you'll never have to endure
another boring chord progression! These additional tones will spice up any progression.
This sequence will give you a chance to combine many of the new chords you have learnt -
experiment with picking each chord as an arpeggio rather than simply strumming.

TRACKS 16+17

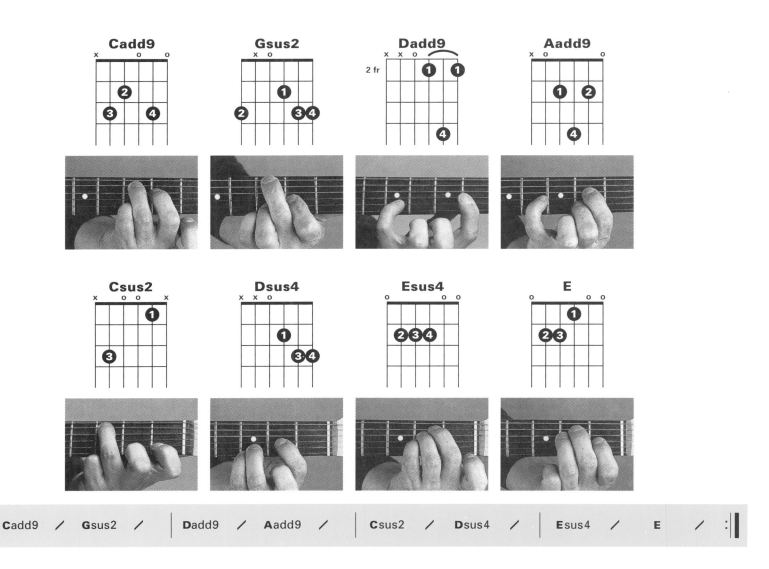

Experiment with these alternative voicings in the example above.

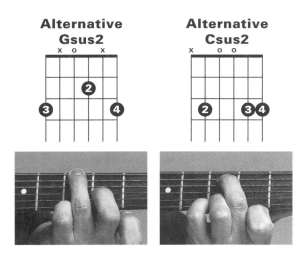

> **JARGON ALERT!**
> Playing an arpeggio simply
> means picking the notes of a
> chord one at a time, rather
> than hitting them all at once.

Adding the 6 and Major 7

There are two more notes from the major scale that we can use to liven up major chords - the 6th and 7th degrees of the scale. Adding these notes produces chords called **6th**s and **major 7th**s - they have a cooler, more mellow feel, in contrast to the expectant mood of **sus2**s and **sus4**s.

Here's the chord box for **C6**:

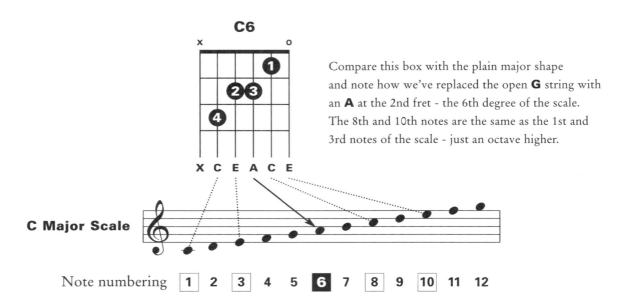

Compare this box with the plain major shape and note how we've replaced the open **G** string with an **A** at the 2nd fret - the 6th degree of the scale. The 8th and 10th notes are the same as the 1st and 3rd notes of the scale - just an octave higher.

The five easiest **6th** shapes are given below:

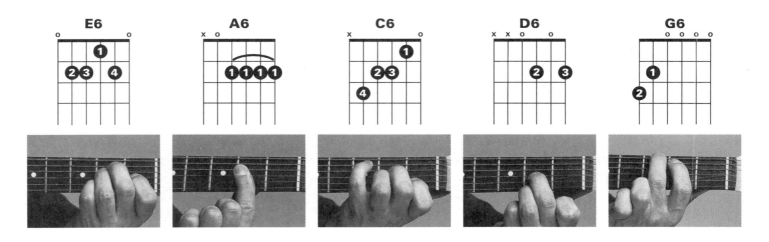

Check out these mellow voicings with the 6th tucked away inside the shape:

SIXTH SENSE
Here are some classic tracks that use the **6**:

'She Loves You'
The Beatles
Check out that last chord!

'Foot Of The Mountain'
Paul Weller

'Love Is The Drug'
Roxy Music

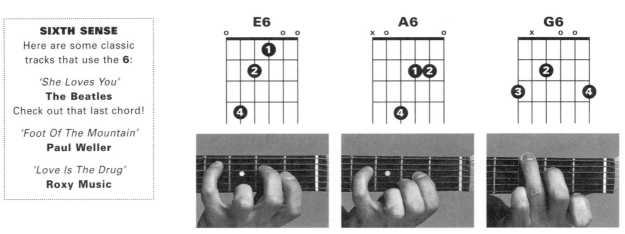

'Sixmania!'

Here's a simple chord sequence using **6th** chords. Listen to the warm flavour of this piece in comparison to the sound of the same piece if played with open major chords, or **sus2/sus4** chords.

TRACKS 18+19

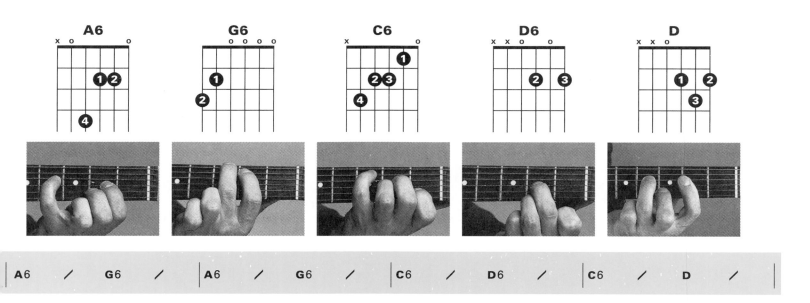

| A6 | / | G6 | / | A6 | / | G6 | / | C6 | / | D6 | / | C6 | / | D | / |

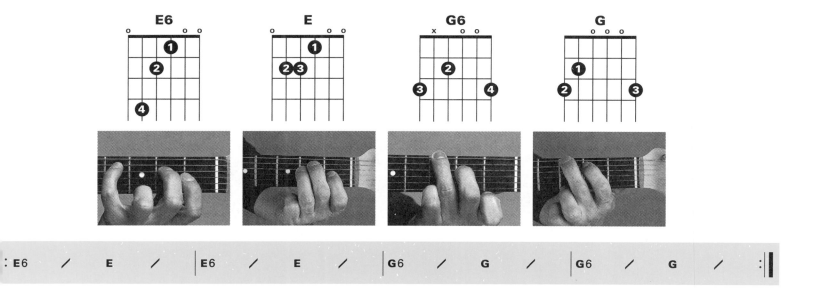

| E6 | / | E | / | E6 | / | E | / | G6 | / | G | / | G6 | / | G | / |

In A Sentimental Mood – The Major 7

Adding a 6th gives a natural warmth to the sound, but leaves the basic feel of the chord unchanged. The **major 7th** (or **maj7**, as it is abbreviated) is more defined and instantly recognisable - think Burt Bacharach or café jazz!

Here's how **Cmaj7** shapes up:

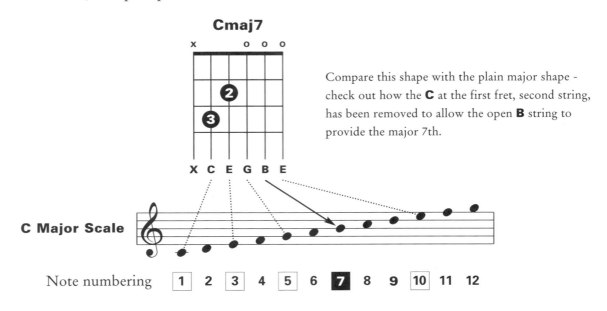

Compare this shape with the plain major shape - check out how the **C** at the first fret, second string, has been removed to allow the open **B** string to provide the major 7th.

And here are the five easiest **maj7** shapes in open positions:

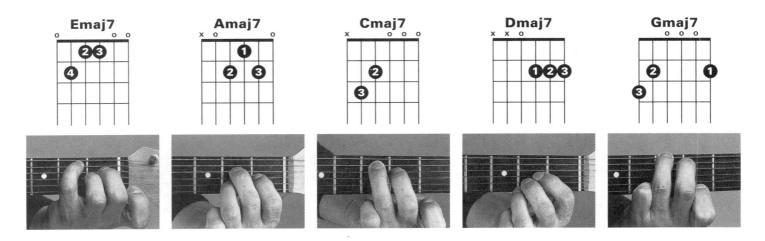

'Mr Cool'

Now it's time to kick back and relax as you amble through this progression of **6th**s and **maj7th**s:

TRACKS 20+21

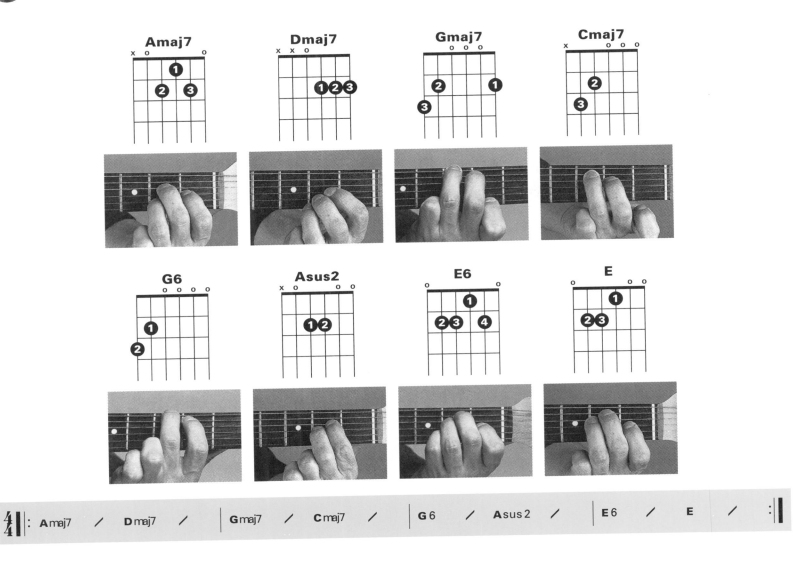

You now know five new ways to jazz up the sound of straightforward, open chords. You can use **sus4**, **sus2**, **add9**, **maj7** and **6th** chords in place of the chords you would usually use. Start experimenting - and listen out for the changes these chords make!

> **MAJOR SONGS - MAJOR 7S!**
>
> *'Design For Life'*
> **Manic Street Preachers**
>
> *'You Are The Sunshine Of My Life'*
> **Stevie Wonder**
>
> *'Girl From Ipanema'*
> **Stan Getz**
>
> *'Raindrops Keep Falling On My Head'*
> from the film
> *'Butch Cassidy and the Sundance Kid'*

3. The Dominant 7th

The **Dominant 7th** is, as its name suggests, one of the most important chords in any guitarist's repertoire - it's instantly recognisable and fundamental to almost every style of popular music.

All the notes we've added to major chords so far have been taken from the major scale - the 2nd, 4th, 6th and 7th degrees. To create the **dominant 7th** we need to take a note that's not found in the major scale - the flattened seventh. Here's the chord shape for **C7**:

SHORT & SWEET
Because the **dominant 7th** is used so frequently, musicians tend to refer to it as just the **7th**. The 'dominant' part of the name is simply left off.

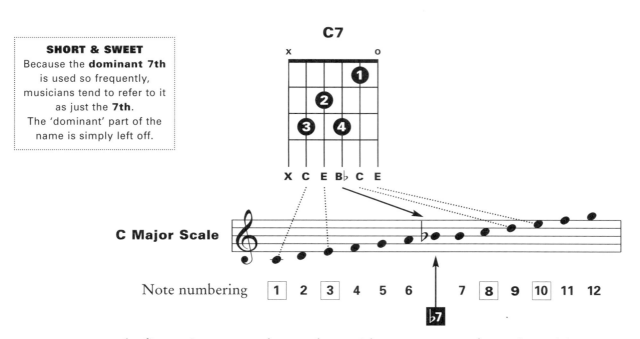

Here are the five easiest **dom7** shapes, along with two common alternative voicings, all in open position:

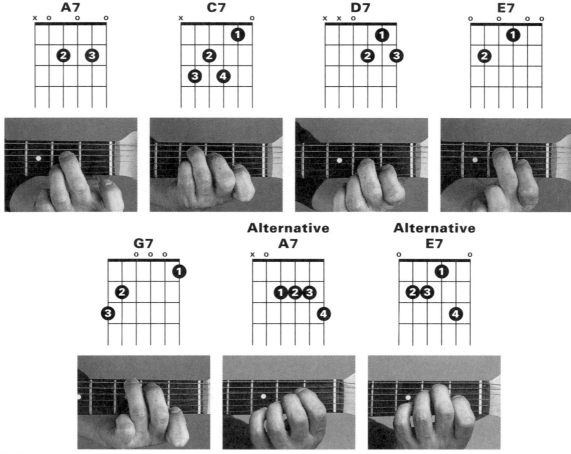

Playing the Blues – using the 7th

Listen to the difference in sound and texture between these two standard 12-bar blues progressions. The first uses 3 of the most common open major chords in a well-known sequence...

12-BAR BLUES
The '12-bar' sequence is possibly the most common chord sequence of all time - and here's the good news - it only uses three chords!

'Straight Ahead'

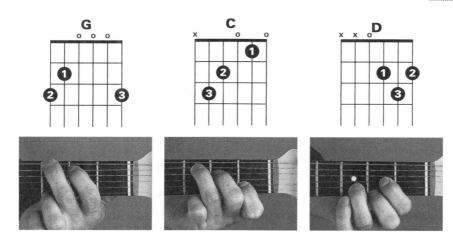

'Seventh Heaven'

Now listen to how the sound of this piece changes simply by replacing all of the open chords with **7**s.

ONE - FOUR - FIVE
All 12-bar sequences are based on the same chord progression, using chords built on the 1st, 4th and 5th degrees of the scale. So these examples in **G** use the chords of **G**, **C** and **D**, while a 12-bar in **E** would use the chords of **E**, **A** and **B**.

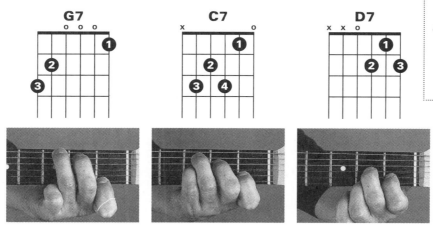

Funk it up – the dominant 9th Chord

We can make these **dominant 7th** chords sound really funky by extending the chord even further and adding the 9th. Here's the chord box for **C9**:

C9

X C E B♭ D E

C Major Scale

Note numbering   1   2   3   4   5   6   7   8   9   10   12   13

♭7

Compare this chord box with the **C7** shape on page 20, and with the **Cadd9** shape on page 10. Effectively, we've combined the two to form **C9** - **C7** doesn't have the 9th degree of the scale, and **Cadd9** doesn't have the seventh, but **C9** has both!

The five easiest **9th** shapes are given below:

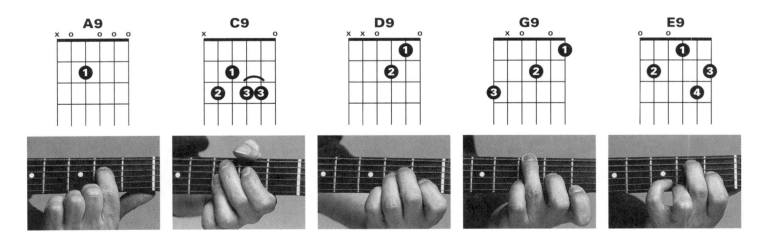

A9   C9   D9   G9   E9

'Living In A Funkytown'

Get down and get funky with this sequence constructed entirely from **9th** and **7th** chords:

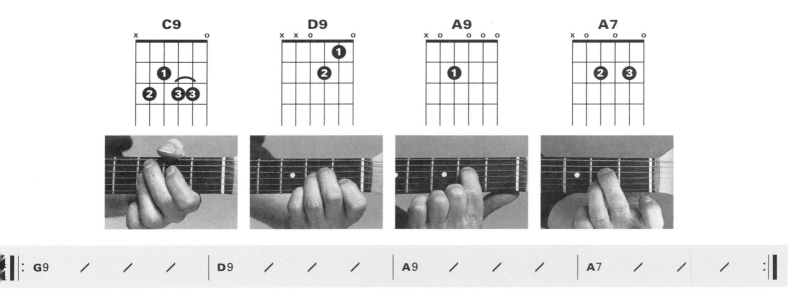

Here's an alternative **C9** voicing using a 3rd finger barre:

TECHNICAL TIP
Because this shape doesn't contain any open strings it is moveable. You can slide the whole shape up two frets to create **D9**. Experiment by playing the **C9** and **D9** chords in *'Living In A Funkytown'* with these new voicings.

TECHNIQUE
Make sure that your 2nd finger remains clear of the 4th string. Use your 2nd finger or left hand thumb to deaden the 6th string.

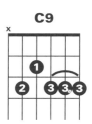

FUNKSTERS WHO USE THE 9TH
James Brown - The King of the funky **9th** chord.
Check out 'Papa's Got A Brand New Bag', or 'I Got You (I Feel Good)'
for the definitive sound of the **9th** in action.

4. Basic Minor Shapes

How are minor chords created?

If you extend the **C** major scale down by two notes you will reach the note of **A**:

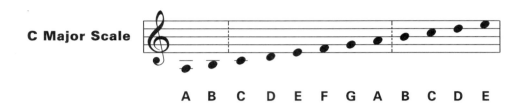

By playing the **C** major scale from **A** to **A** (instead of from **C** to **C**) we create a new scale, called **A natural minor**.

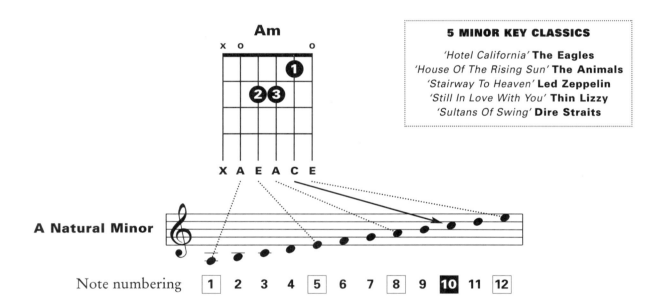

5 MINOR KEY CLASSICS

'Hotel California' **The Eagles**
'House Of The Rising Sun' **The Animals**
'Stairway To Heaven' **Led Zeppelin**
'Still In Love With You' **Thin Lizzy**
'Sultans Of Swing' **Dire Straits**

Just like the major chord, we create a minor chord by using the 1st, 3rd and 5th degrees of the scale. So what's the difference between major and minor?

The answer lies in the **3rd note** of the scales:

In a major scale, the 3rd note is two tones (4 frets) above the root note and is called the major 3rd.

In a minor scale, the 3rd note is 1½ tones (3 frets) above the root note and is called the minor 3rd.

Basic Minor Chord Shapes

In addition to the 5 basic major open chord shapes we discussed in Chapter 1, you probably also know some of these open minor shapes:

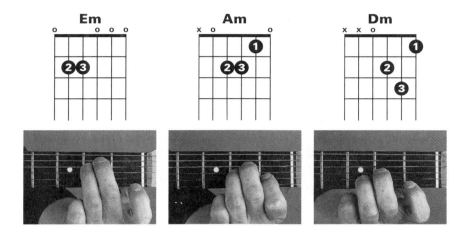

Make sure you are familiar with these minor chords.

> **C MINOR & G MINOR**
> The two other common minor shapes: **Cm** and **Gm** – require a barre. We'll be looking at those later...

'Minor Bird'

Minor chords create a sad, melancholy mood. This example will give you the opportunity to use all three of the open minor chord shapes that you already know.

TRACKS 28+29

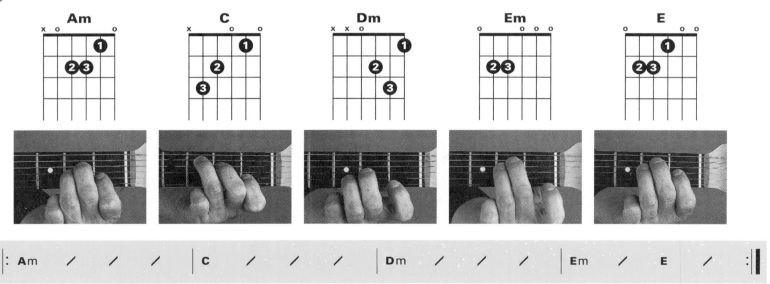

5. Altering Minor Shapes

So, how do we spice up these basic minor chords?

The first thing that you can try is to combine them with **sus** chords. Remember - **sus** chords are neither major nor minor because the all-important 3rd degree of the scale has been replaced by either the 2nd or the 4th. **Sus 2**s and **Sus 4**s can resolve to either minor or major chords.

'Don't Leave Me In Suspense'

This example shows how **sus2** and **sus4** can resolve to simple major and minor chords.

TRACKS 30+31

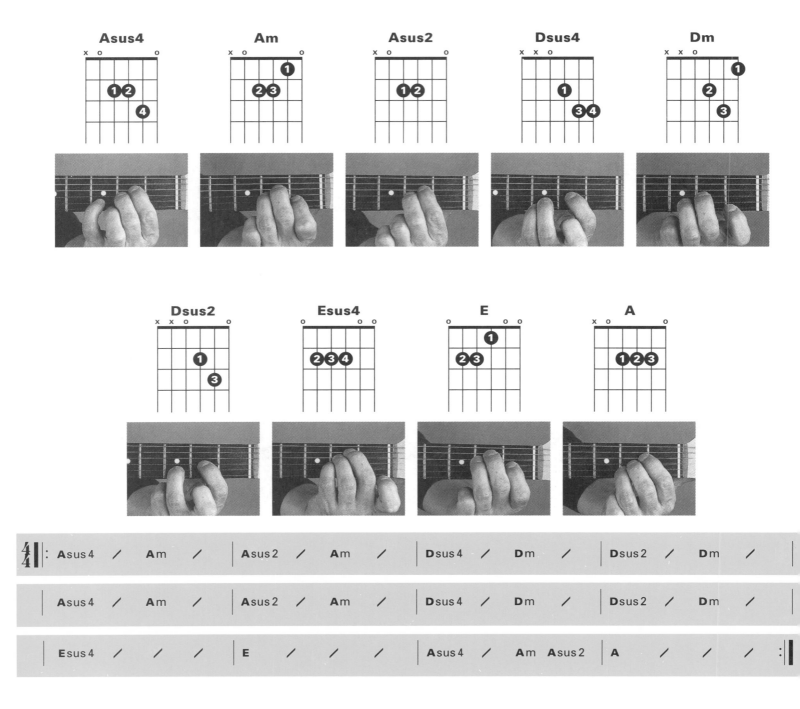

Smooth & soulful – minor 7 chords

We can also add notes to the basic minor shapes. For example, if we add the 7th note from the natural minor scale, we create the chord of **Am7**:

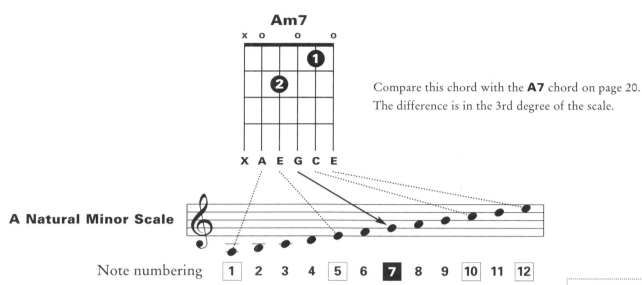

Compare this chord with the **A7** chord on page 20. The difference is in the 3rd degree of the scale.

Here are some more easy **minor 7th** chord shapes:

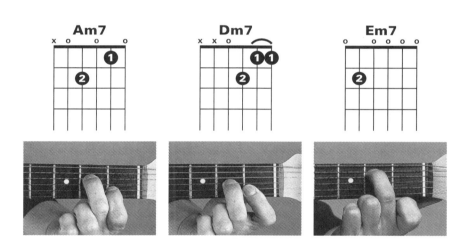

TECHNICAL TIP
The 7th note in the natural minor scale is a whole tone (2 frets) below the root note - just like the flattened 7th in the **dominant 7th** chords you played on page 20. In the major scale the 7th degree is only a semitone (1 fret) below the root note.

These alternative voicings have the 7th note placed higher within the chord.

'Seven Seas'

Minor 7th chords have a more laid-back sound than straight minor triads. Listen to the sound of the chords in this straightforward minor progression...

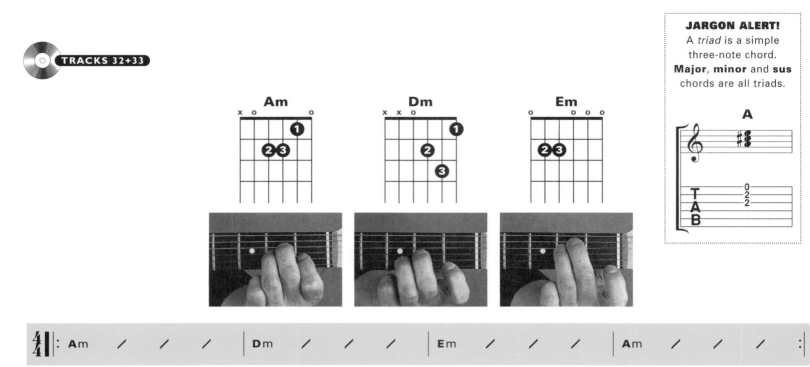

'The Magnificent Seven'

Now check out how we can make the same straight-forward minor progression sound much more sophisticated by turning all the minor chords into **minor 7ths**.

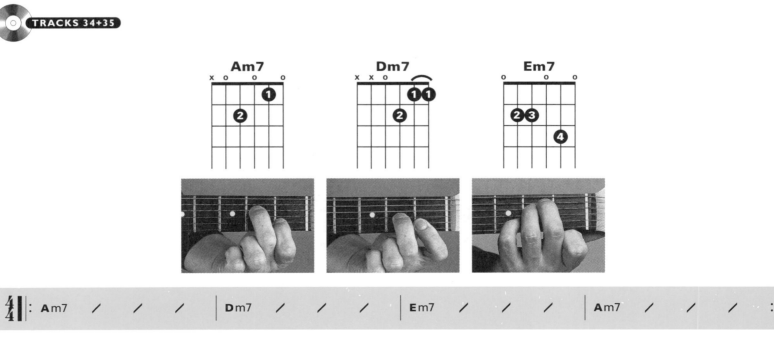

The Minor Major 7th

Here's a strange-sounding chord name – the **m(maj7th)**! Pronounced "minor major 7th" this chord consists of a minor triad plus the major 7th.

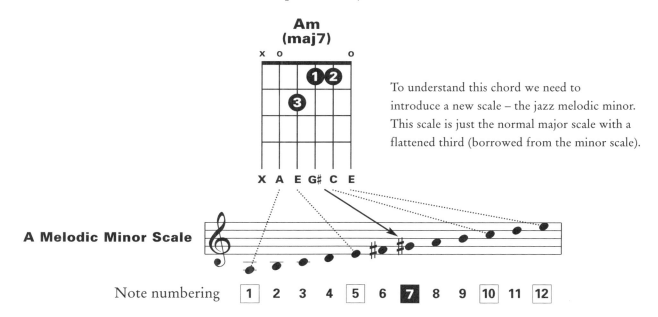

Am (maj7)

X A E G# C E

A Melodic Minor Scale

Note numbering   1 2 3 4 5 6 7 8 9 10 11 12

To understand this chord we need to introduce a new scale – the jazz melodic minor. This scale is just the normal major scale with a flattened third (borrowed from the minor scale).

Here are three easy **m(maj7th)** shapes:

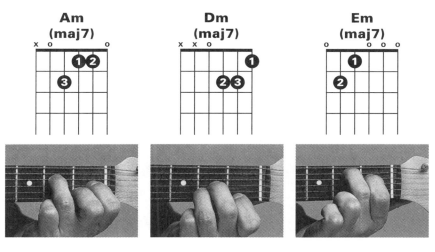

Am (maj7)   **Dm (maj7)**   **Em (maj7)**

THE JAZZ MELODIC MINOR
Like the **minor 7th**, the **m(maj7th)** consists of the 1st, 3rd, 5th and 7th notes from its parent scale. The difference is that the jazz melodic minor has a major 7th, whereas the natural minor has a flattened 7th.

TRACKS 36+37

'In Tents'

The **m(maj7th)** has a tense, but melancholy flavour - the result of its combination of minor and major influences. Check it out in this chord sequence:

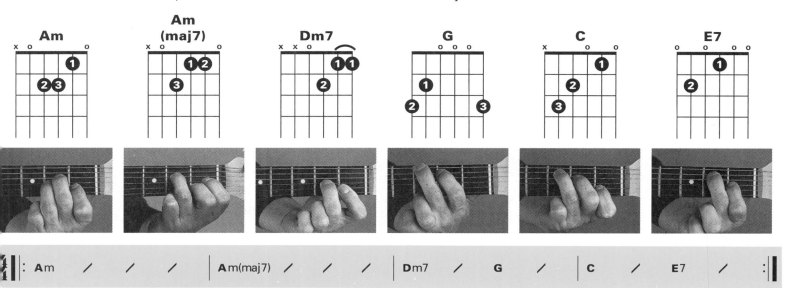

Am   **Am (maj7)**   **Dm7**   **G**   **C**   **E7**

‖: Am / / / | Am(maj7) / / / | Dm7 / G / | C / E7 / :‖

Minor 6th

We can create another exotic sounding chord using the jazz melodic minor scale.

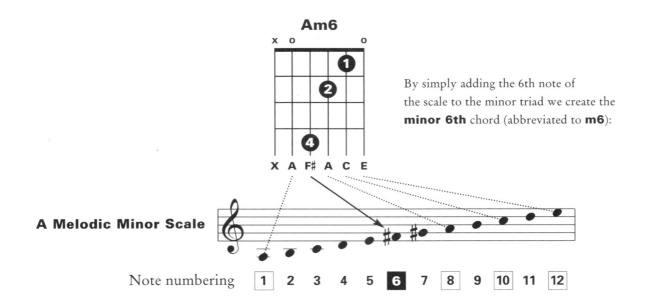

By simply adding the 6th note of the scale to the minor triad we create the **minor 6th** chord (abbreviated to **m6**):

Here are the three easiest **minor 6th** shapes, plus an alternative shape for **Em6**:

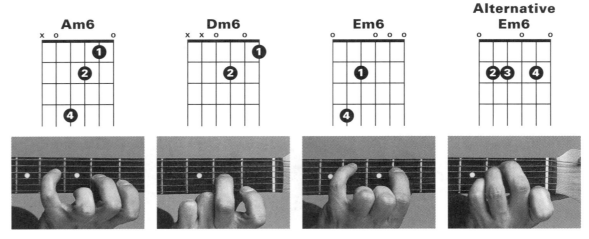

TRACKS 38+39

'On The Move'

In this next example, listen out for the melodic movement created by the changing chords:

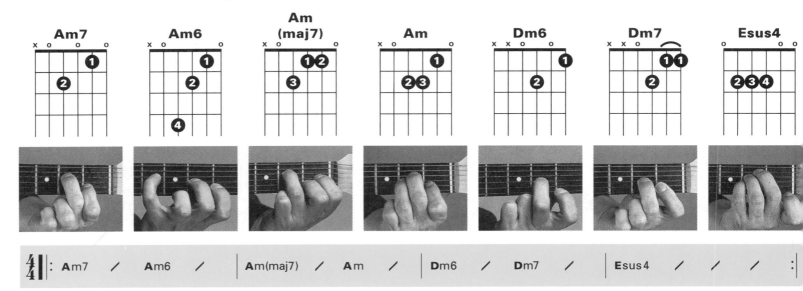

A Classic Chord Sequence

We'll finish our look at altering minor chords with a classic descending sequence.

'The Descending Miner'

By combining the **m(maj7th)**, the **minor 7th** and the **minor 6th** chords in a sequence, you can create one of the most recognisable chord sequences in the world!

> **THE M(MAJ7TH) IN ACTION**
> The **m(maj7)/m7/m6** sequence was used heavily by The Beatles. Check out some of these...
> *'Michelle'*
> *'While My Guitar Gently Weeps'*
> *'Something'*
> *'I Me Mine'*

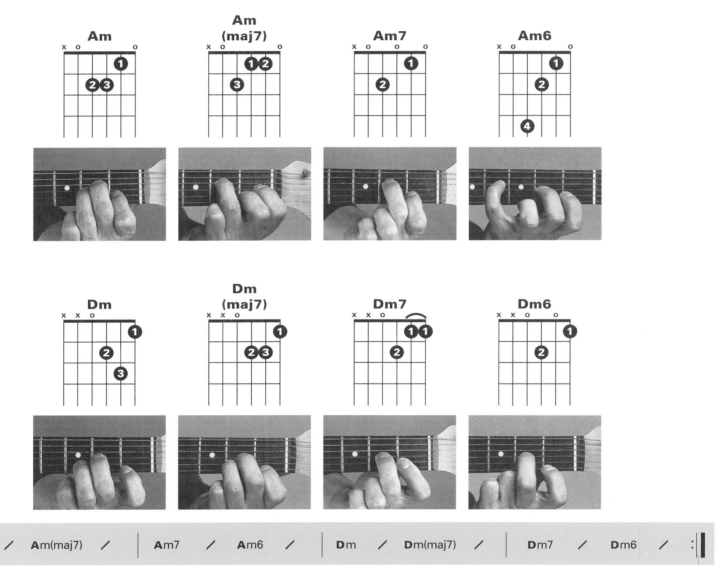

Next time you find yourself playing a simple minor chord for a few bars, inject some life and movement with these altered minor chords.

That's **Chord Chemistry!**

6. So Far, So Good

So, what have I learned so far? sus2 and sus4

You can add tension and movement to major and minor chords by temporarily substituting them with **sus2** and **sus4** chords.

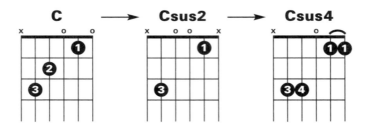

add9, maj7, dom7 and 9

You can change the mood of a major chord sequence by adding notes to create **add9**, **maj7**, **dominant 7** and **9** chords.

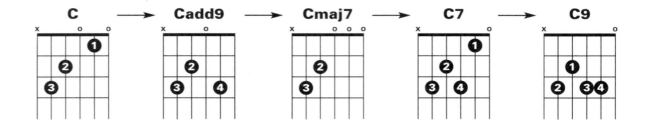

minor7 and minor6

You can apply exactly the same idea to minor chords to create **minor 7ths**, **m(maj7ths)** and **minor 6ths**.

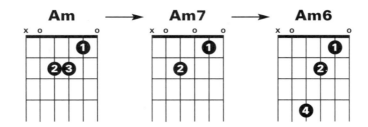

So, Chord Chemists, it's time to start experimenting!

Let's take some simple chord progressions and add some magic by introducing some of these new chords. Let's start with a standard two chord progression that you'll find in many songs.

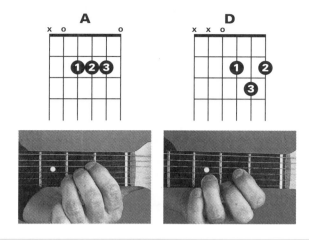

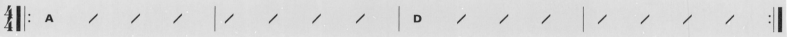

'Why Use Two, When Eight Will Do!'

Now let's try this version - with added 'Chord Chemistry'! Listen for the melodic movement created by the chord changes, and compare the sound to the previous simple 2-chord sequence.

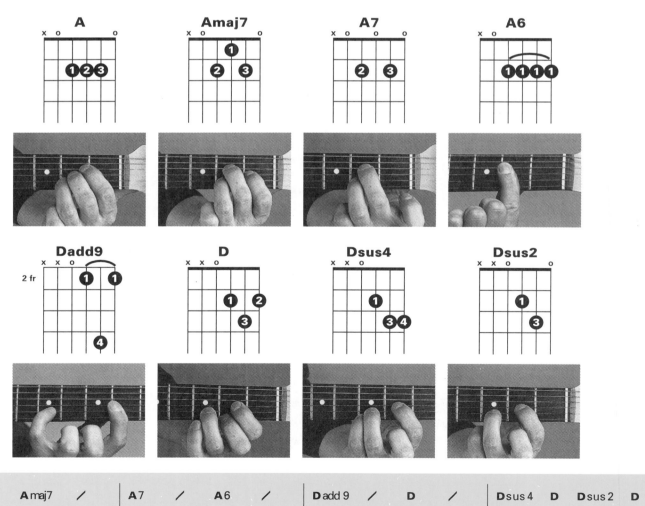

'Four-Bar Ballad'

If you refer back to page 21, you'll remember that the 12-bar blues is a classic sequence based on chords I, IV and V. Well, here's a common rock'n'roll ballad chord sequence that adds chord VI to form the sequence, I, VI, IV, V.

If you refer back to page 21

🔘 **TRACKS 44+45**

TECHNICAL TIP
This example is in a slow **12/8** tempo. It's often useful to think of **12/8** as a slow four-in-a-bar, where each beat is divided into 3. Try counting "**1**-2-3, **2**-2-3, **3**-2-3, **4**-2-3" as you play.

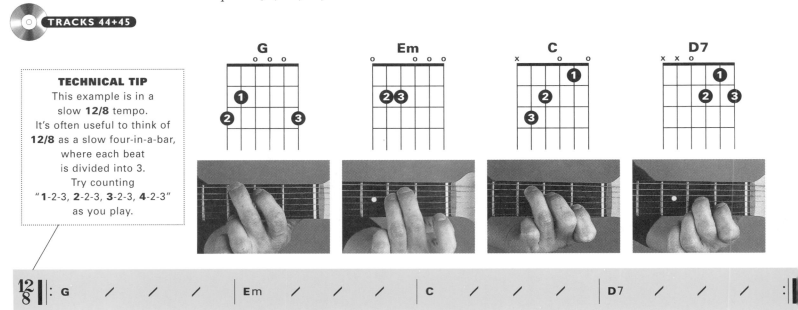

$\frac{12}{8}$ ‖: G / / / | Em / / / | C / / / | D7 / / / :‖

'Teen Queen'

Now let's liven up the sequence with some Chord Chemistry! Sounds better, doesn't it? Try picking separate notes rather than simply strumming the chord.

🔘 **TRACKS 46+47**

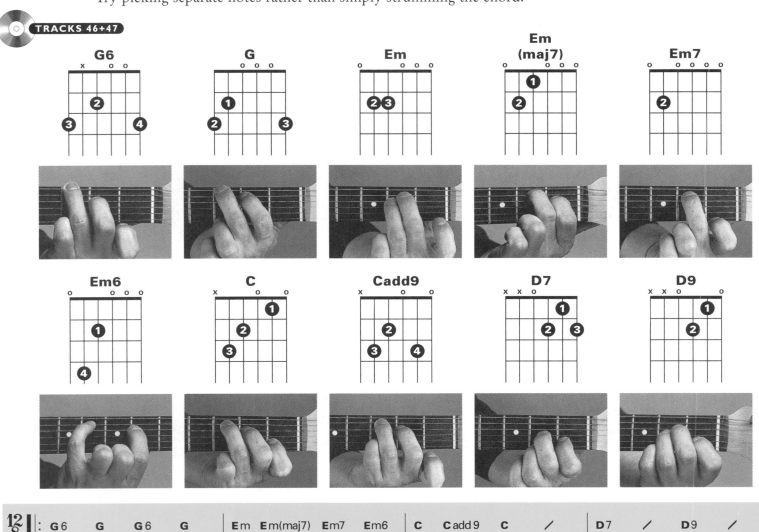

$\frac{12}{8}$ ‖: G6 G G6 G | Em Em(maj7) Em7 Em6 | C Cadd9 C / | D7 / D9 / :‖

7. Slash Chords

Root Notes

Before we can look at slash chords, you need to understand the concept of root notes.

The root note of a chord is the note that shares its name with the chord. So, the root note of **C major** is **C** and the root note of **G minor** is **G**, and so on.

Most of the time, the root note is the bass note of the chord. However, we can specify different bass notes by using slash chords.

For example: **C/E** means a **C major** chord with an **E** as the bass note.

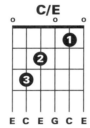 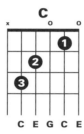

Can you hear the difference between **C** and **C/E**? Go back to page 9 and play 'Spice It Up' again - listen out for the **G/B** chord in that sequence, it's another first inversion chord.

Inversions

The number of inversions of any chord is the same as the number of notes in that chord. For example, the chord of **Cmaj7** uses four notes from its parent scale - the 1st, 3rd, 5th and 7th. This gives us four possible bass notes:

CLASSIC BASS LINES
These three classic songs all have prominent moving bass lines:

'Changingman'
Paul Weller

'Something'
The Beatles

'Stairway To Heaven'
Led Zeppelin

C in the bass - root position: **Cmaj7**

E in the bass - 1st inversion: **Cmaj7/E**

G in the bass - 2nd inversion: **Cmaj7/G**

B in the bass - 3rd inversion: **Cmaj7/B**

THEORY TIP
Chords with the root note in the bass are called root position chords. They sound resolved and 'at rest'.

C/E is an example of a first inversion chord – instead of using the root note as the bass note, we've chosen the next chord tone (the 3rd note of the scale).

First inversion chords generate a sense of movement - they always want to progress on to the next chord.

Moving Bass Lines

Slash chords are particularly useful for creating moving bass lines.
Have a look at these classic progressions:

'Forward Slash'

Slash chords are particularly useful for creating moving bass lines. Have a look at these classic progressions. Here, the bass line is rising, making the track sound like it's moving forward.

TRACKS 48+49

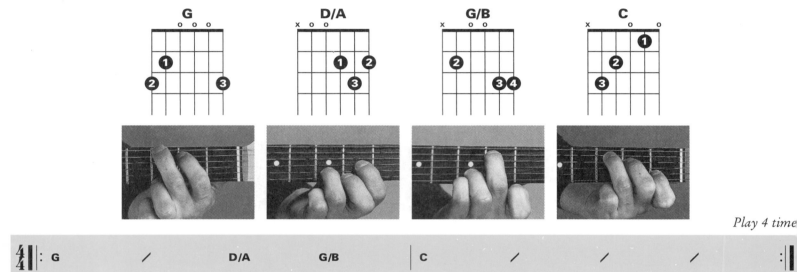

Play 4 time

'Back Slash'

In this second chord progression the bass line is moving down the scale from **G**, creating a completely different feel to the piece.

TRACKS 50+51

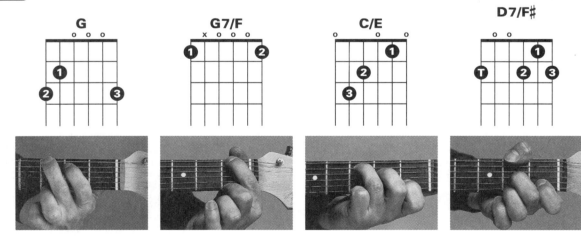

Play 4 time

All the slash chords you've used so far have used chord tones as the bass note, but there's no reason why the bass note has to be a note from within the chord.

Now let's experiment! We'll take a basic **D major** chord and create new chords simply by adding different bass notes:

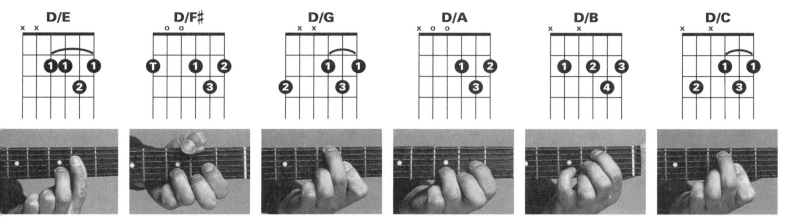

To finish off, let's take another look at '*The Descending Miner*', which you first encountered on page 31. This time we'll put the descending movement in the bass:

'The Descending Miner (Slight Return)'

TRACKS 52+53

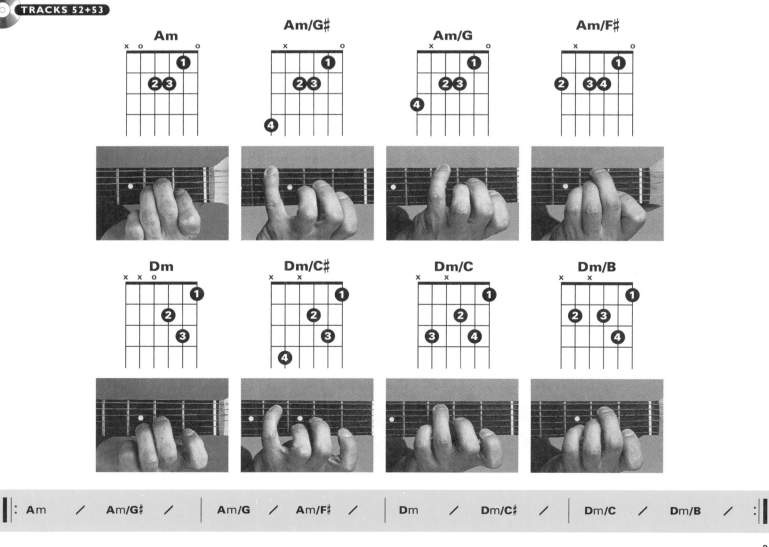

8. Let It Ring!

Here's a great way to make any chord sequence sound good – just make sure that all the chords you use share common notes (these shared chord tones can also be called pedal notes).

Here's a fairly ordinary sequence:

'Plain Sailing'

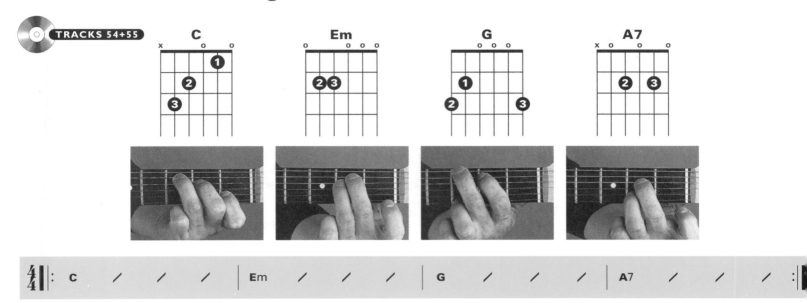

'Keep Pedalling!'

...but using a little Chord Chemistry we can come up with this more interesting sequence which uses the **add9**, **m7**, **6** and **7sus4** chords. Listen to the difference between the way these examples sound.

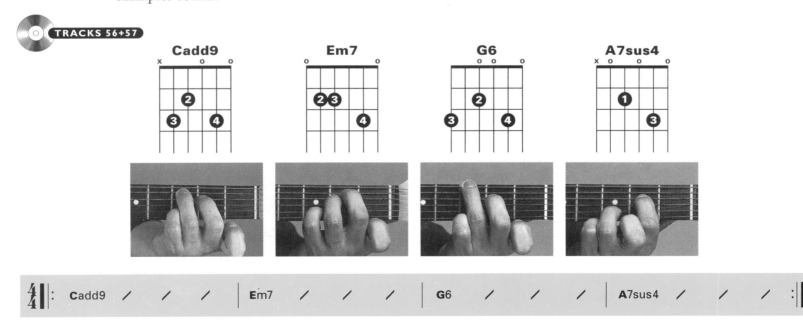

The sequence immediately sounds much more interesting, because all of these chord shapes include two common tones - the open **E** string, and the **D** on the 2nd string.

'Pedalo Flamenco'

Another easy way of creating exciting sounds is to move open chord shapes up the neck, allowing the open strings to ring on as pedal notes. This example uses the **E major** shape and has a Spanish flavour.

TRACKS 58+59

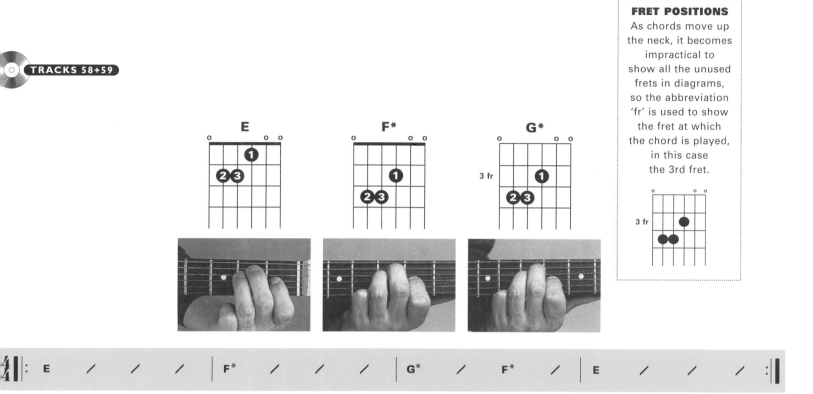

FRET POSITIONS
As chords move up the neck, it becomes impractical to show all the unused frets in diagrams, so the abbreviation 'fr' is used to show the fret at which the chord is played, in this case the 3rd fret.

So, what are these chords called?

Chords like these can be difficult to name - let's look at the **F*** chord as an example:

The pedal notes are the open **E** and **B** strings. **E** is the **major 7th** from the **F major** scale - that's one piece of information you'll need to include in the chord name. The **B** is slightly more tricky - the **F major** scale contains a **B♭** as the fourth tone; so to get **B** natural we need to sharpen the fourth degree of the scale. When naming chords we always add notes from outside the original octave so we call this **add♯11**.

So the basic name for this shape is **Fmaj7add♯11**.

However, the open bottom **E** string is also ringing out under the other chord tones – we can use slash notation to represent this.

The correct name for this chord is **Fmaj7add♯11/E**. Quite a mouthful for such an easy shape! You might find it easier to just think of these chords as altered versions of the basic major shapes.

'Half Time'

Here's another example using common chord tones - this time it's a **G** on the top string and **D** on the second string that ring out throughout the sequence.

'WONDERWALL BY OASIS is a classic example of this style. If you listen carefully, you'll hear that the tension in the verse is resolved in the chorus by reverting to the usual chord voicings.

 TRACKS 60+61

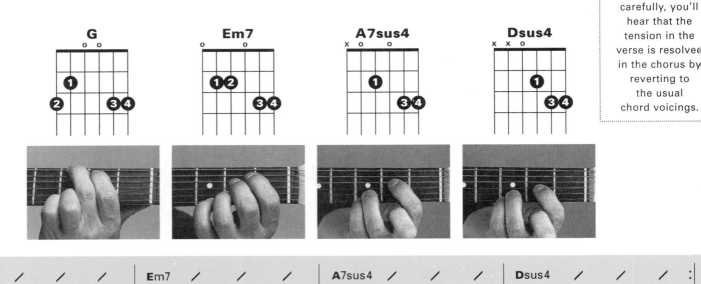

Hearing the chords changing around these constant notes creates a mild tension that demands the listener's attention.

'Back To My Roots'

This example is similar to 'Pedalo Flamenco' - you're simply moving the basic chord shape up and down the neck, but this time also adding the root note of the chord on the bottom **E** string.

TRACKS 62+63

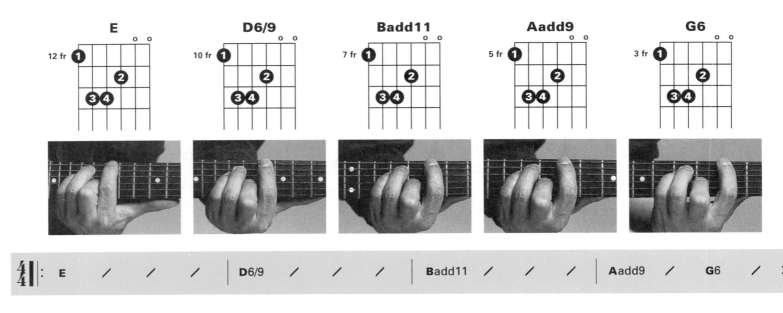

Try experimenting with this technique using other open chord shapes such as **A** and **D** and see what sounds you can create!

9. Moveable Chords

Using a Capo

You've now explored a wealth of different chord types in some of the most common keys. But what about awkward keys like **B♭** and **C♯**?

One approach would be to use a capo and stick with your familiar open chord shapes. For example, if you put your capo on the first fret and play the open **A major** shape, you will actually produce a chord of **B♭**.

A far more versatile approach is to use moveable chords. To start with, let's look at barre chords. A barre is produced by one finger pressing down two or more strings (you may remember this from page 7). Here are four practical shapes that can be moved anywhere on the fretboard, because they don't contain any open strings.

E shape

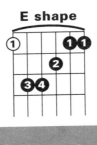

A shape

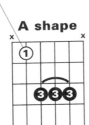

C shape

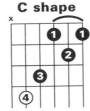

D shape

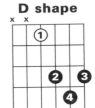

Secondly, you'll need to learn (or be able to work out) the letter names of every note on the 4th, 5th and 6th strings. These diagrams give you all the information you need:

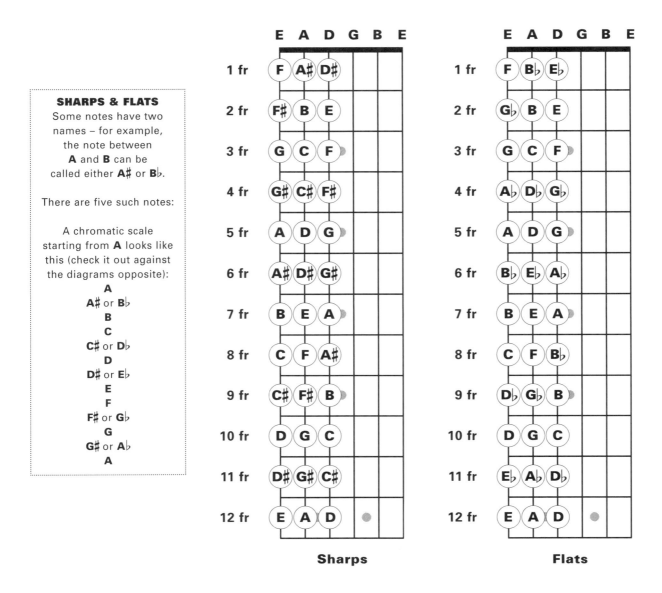

Sharps & Flats diagrams

Sharps (left diagram) — strings labeled E A D G B E:

fr	E	A	D
1 fr	F	A♯	D♯
2 fr	F♯	B	E
3 fr	G	C	F
4 fr	G♯	C♯	F♯
5 fr	A	D	G
6 fr	A♯	D♯	G♯
7 fr	B	E	A
8 fr	C	F	A♯
9 fr	C♯	F♯	B
10 fr	D	G	C
11 fr	D♯	G♯	C♯
12 fr	E	A	D

Sharps

Flats (right diagram) — strings labeled E A D G B E:

fr	E	A	D
1 fr	F	B♭	E♭
2 fr	G♭	B	E
3 fr	G	C	F
4 fr	A♭	D♭	G♭
5 fr	A	D	G
6 fr	B♭	E♭	A♭
7 fr	B	E	A
8 fr	C	F	B♭
9 fr	D♭	G♭	B
10 fr	D	G	C
11 fr	E♭	A♭	D♭
12 fr	E	A	D

Flats

Try picking notes at random and working out their names. If necessary, you can start at the open string and work up the chromatic scale until you reach the fret you've picked.

Here are some examples of the four barre chord shapes we looked at earlier, check the root notes against the sharp and flat diagrams above:

G chord using E shape — 3 fr

D♯ chord using A shape — 6 fr

F chord using C shape — 8 fr

B♭ chord using D shape — 8 fr

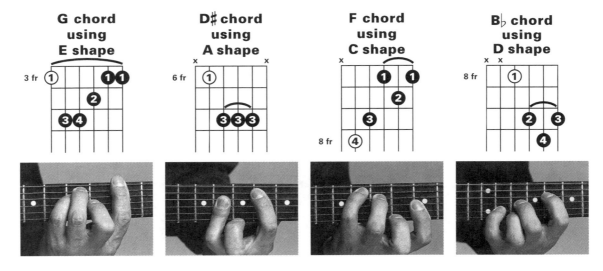

'Barre Crawl'

Here are two sets of shapes that can be used to play this sequence – experiment and find other combinations of shapes that you can use.

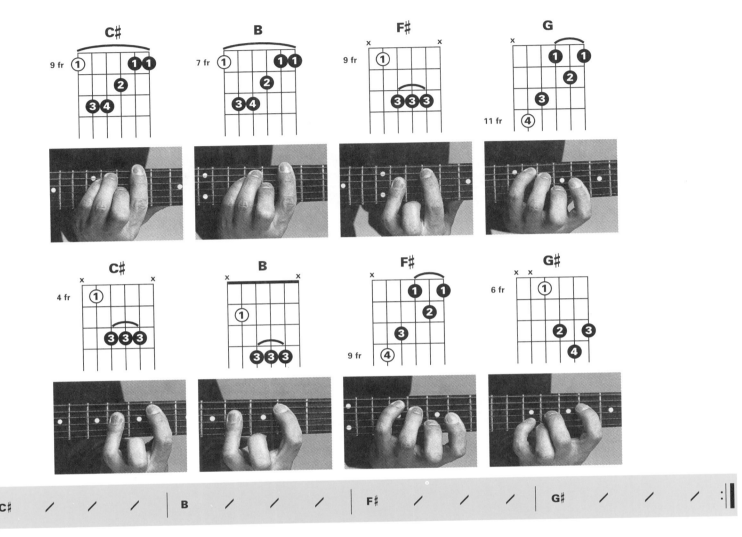

Moveable A shapes

You can alter barre chords to create all the variations that we've already discussed. However, to keep the shape moveable you'll have to avoid open strings – this can make some voicings quite tricky! Let's look at the **A** shape:

> **TECHNICAL TIP**
> The third finger barre has been included in the **sus4** shape to make it easier to resolve to the major chord.

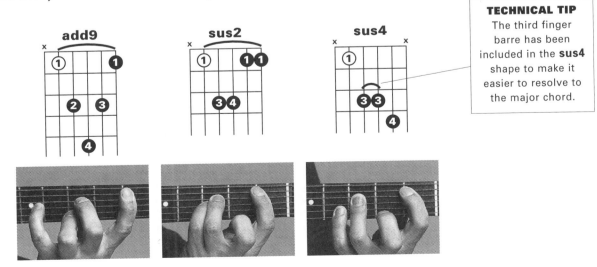

Altering Moveable Shapes

Moveable chords don't necessarily have to include a barre – here are some moveable versions of the **maj7**, **dom7** and **6** shapes we discussed earlier:

TECHNIQUE TIP
Take care to mute unwanted strings. The sixth string can be deadened with the left hand thumb or tip of the first finger, and you can use the fourth finger to deaden the first string.

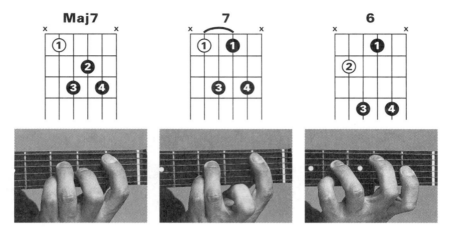

Moveable E shapes

Some moveable shapes lend themselves more readily to certain altered chords. Here are some common **E** shape voicings:

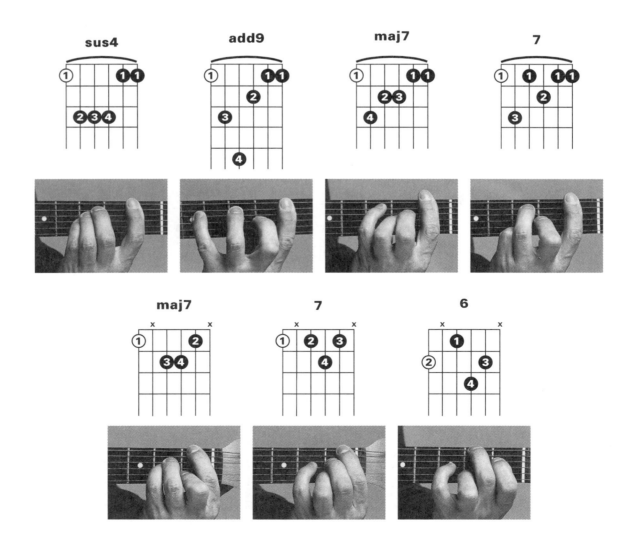

Moveable D Shapes

Here are some useful voicings based on the **D** shape:

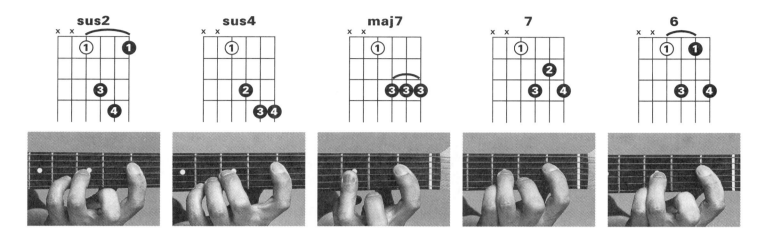

'Second Chance'

Now let's go back and have another look at "Lucky Dip" on page 15. The version below uses only moveable chord voicings, so you can now play this sequence in any key! Some of these voicings require a bit of a stretch - try practising them higher up the neck where the frets are closer together.

TRACKS 66+67

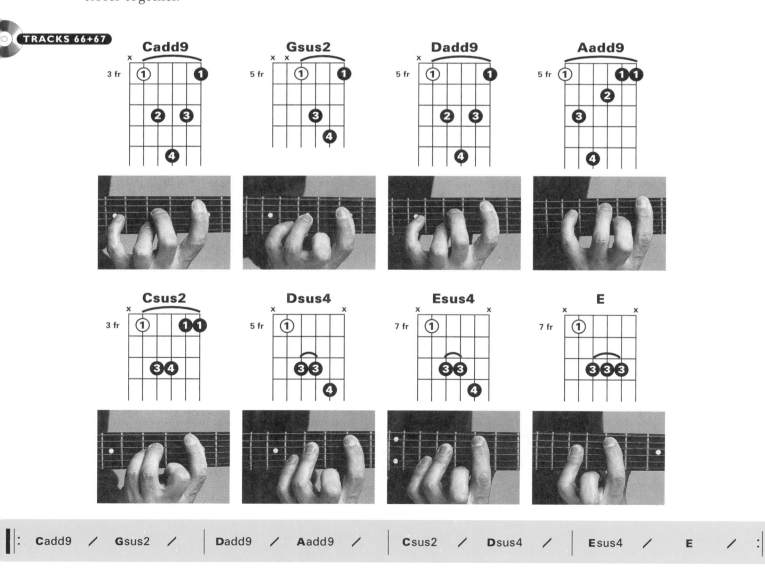

| Cadd9 / Gsus2 / | Dadd9 / Aadd9 / | Csus2 / Dsus4 / | Esus4 / E / |

Moveable C shapes

The **C** shape doesn't really lend itself to much alteration – these are the best two moveable shapes:

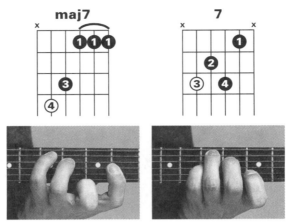

A classic moveable shape – the 7♯9

The **7♯9** shape is a jazz chord that's favoured by rockers and bluesmen alike. Compare the sound of the straight **9**th chord that we introduced on page 22 to the **7♯9** chord, and then check out the funky sound of the next sequence.

JIMI HENDRIX...
used the **7♯9** chord on many of his most famous recordings, such as 'Purple Haze'.

Bluesmen such as Robert Cray and Stevie Ray Vaughan have also used it to great effect.

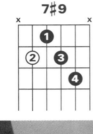

'Sharpen Up'

TRACKS 68+69

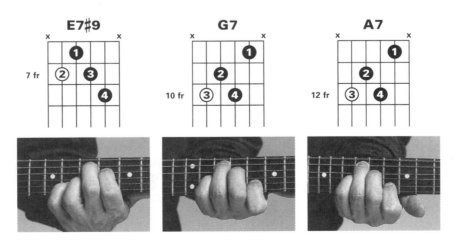

4/4 ‖: E7♯9 / / / / / / / | G7 / / / / | A7 / / / :‖

10. Moveable Minor Chords

Now that you've explored the world of moveable major chords, it's time to do exactly the same thing for the minor shapes.

Basic Moveable Shapes

Here are the three basic moveable minor shapes:

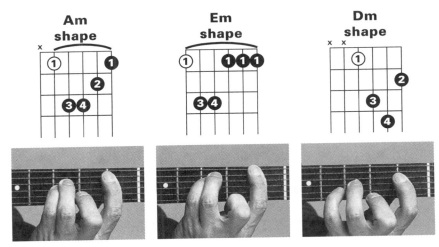

The **Em** shape has its root on the 6th string, the **Am** root can be found on the 5th string and the **Dm** shape has its root on the 4th string. Refer back to the diagram on page 42 to work out the name of any minor chord on the neck.

Moveable A minor shapes

Here are the most common altered voicings for the **Am** shape:

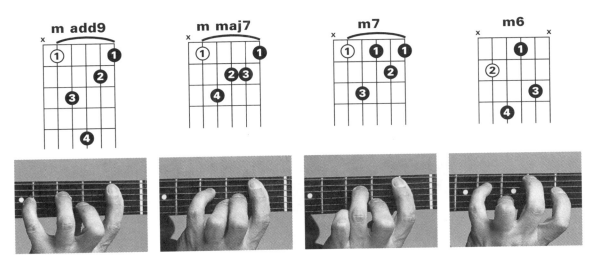

Compare the first three of these chords with the **maj7**, **dom7** and **6** chords based on the **E major** shape on page 44 – these three minor chords are exactly the same shapes moved across one string!

Moveable Minor Shapes Without A Barre

Here are non-barre versions of the last three chords of the **Am** shapes on
the previous page.

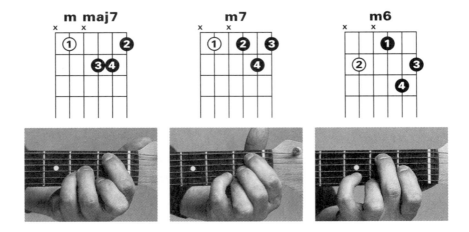

Moveable E minor shapes

Here are some of the most versatile **Em** moveable chord shapes:

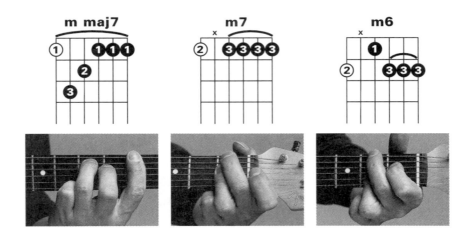

Moveable D minor shapes

And here are the **Dm** shapes:

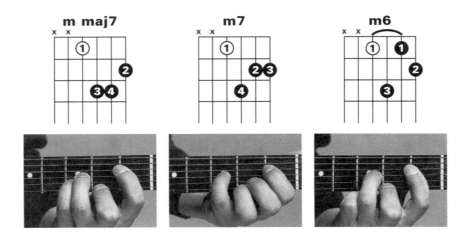

'Miner At The Barre'

Now let's practise the descending sequence you first came across on page 31, 'Descending Miner', but this time using moveable chord shapes.

TRACKS 70+71

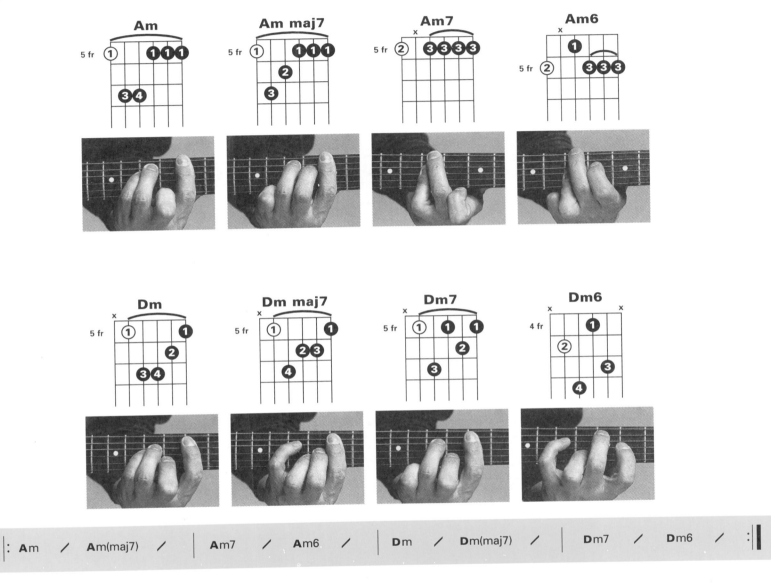

Transposition!

Armed with your knowledge of the moveable shapes listed above, you should now be able to play this example in any key you want! Try working out the positions of the chords for the following sequence, it's simply 'Miner At The Barre' moved from the key of **A minor** to **C minor**.

11. Partial Chords

When you're playing with a band it's often preferable to play partial voicings - these are shapes that only use a few strings.

The most harmonically basic voicing is the power chord (sometimes known as the **5** chord). It only has two notes - the root and 5th notes of its parent scale. Because a power chord doesn't have a third, it isn't major or minor.

Here are the three most useful power chords:

TECHNICAL TIP
Try lightly muting the strings with your right hand while playing power chords to get a chunky rock sound.

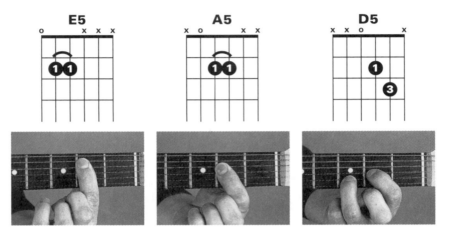

The following voicings are all moveable, and in each case the root note can be found on the lowest string played:

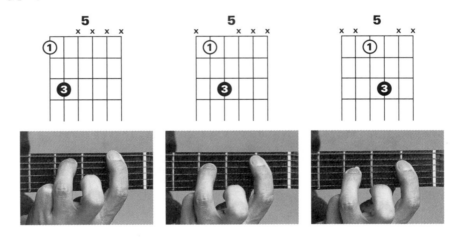

These voicings can be "beefed up" by adding the root note an octave higher:

LET'S ROCK!
Led Zeppelin, Deep Purple, Thin Lizzy, AC/DC and Metallica have all used power chords to create their classic heavy rock tracks.

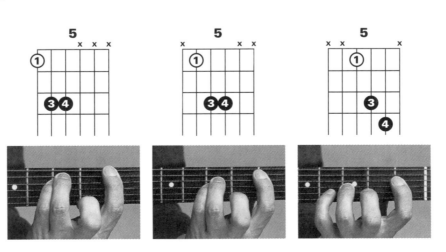

'Power Crazy'

Here's a classic rock sequence that sounds great when played with power chords.
There are two different voicings for each chord - try mixing them up to find a pattern that works
best on the fretboard for you.

 **TRACKS 72+73**

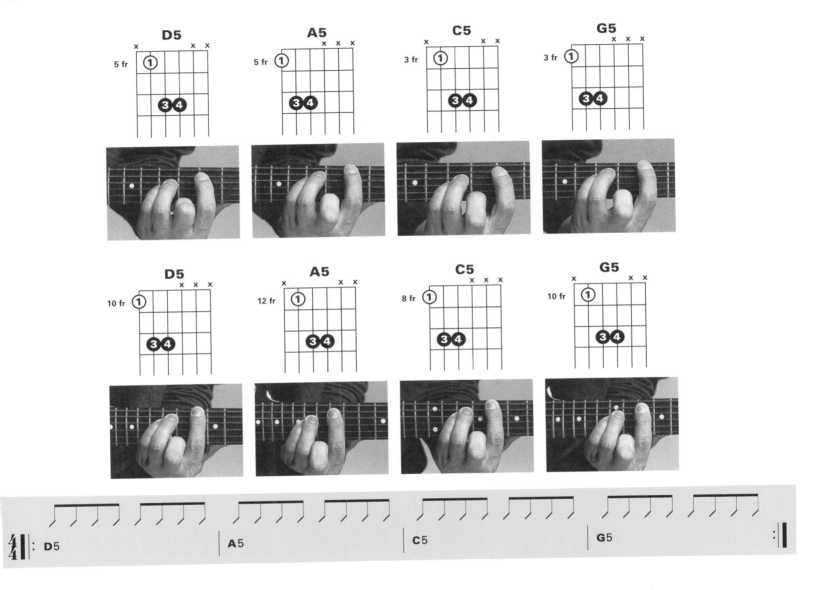

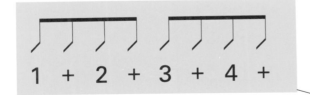

RHYTHM NOTATION:
The rhythm notation in this
example shows there are eight
quaver notes in each bar.
Each beat has two quaver notes,
so you can count it like this....

1 + 2 + 3 + 4 +

for + most people say 'and'.

Jazz Voicings

In jazz, where chords sometimes consist of 5 or 6 different notes, it can be physically impossible to play them all. A jazz guitarist will often pick the most appropriate (or interesting) notes and just play a partial version of the full chord.

Reggae and funk are two other styles of popular music where guitarists favour partial voicings, in this case however, it is to create a percussive sound.

'Funky Village'

Let's have another look at '*Living In A Funky Town*' from page 23.
This time let's use some small, high voicings:

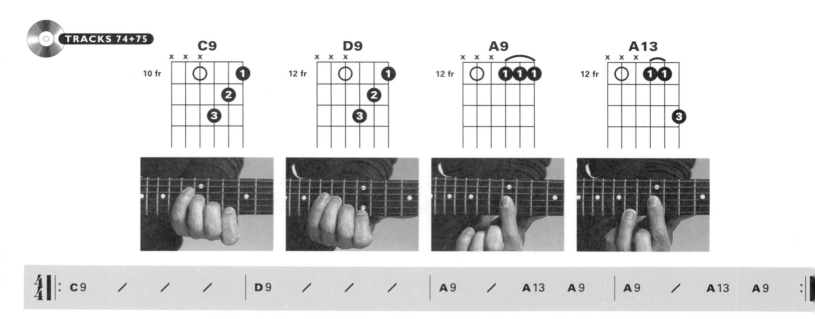

Where's the Root?

Some partial chords don't contain root notes, but you'll still need a reference point when deciding where to position these chords to create the chord you want. Look out for this symbol: ○ – it denotes the position of the root note that would appear in a fuller version of the chords.

It contains no finger number as it is not actually played - it's just there to help you keep track of what chords you are playing!

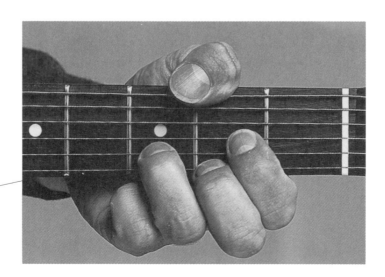

TECHNIQUE TIP
Damp unwanted strings by hanging your left hand thumb over the top of the neck.

Minor Triad Shapes

One really useful thing about partial chords is that one shape can often be used in several different contexts. The minor triad is particularly adaptable - the following five chords share the same notes and fingering, but will produce different results depending on the context in which they appear.

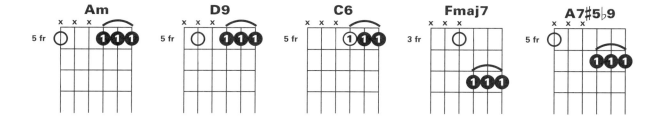

It's worth taking a little time to study the root notes and chord tones so that you understand why the chords are named as they are. Always relate the chord tones to the parent scale, for example, the **Am** chord should be related to the **A** minor scale, and the **Fmaj7** chord to the **F major** scale. Don't be scared of the **A7♯5♭9**, shown above.

Oh, all right then! We'll work through that one with you.

The parent scale is **A major**:

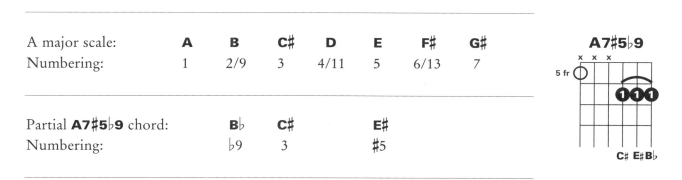

A major scale:	A	B	C♯	D	E	F♯	G♯
Numbering:	1	2/9	3	4/11	5	6/13	7

Partial **A7♯5♭9** chord:	B♭	C♯	E♯
Numbering:	♭9	3	♯5

Remember - this is a partial chord, so you don't need to play *all* the notes.

Who said jazz chords are difficult to play?!

Here are some other useful minor triad shapes:

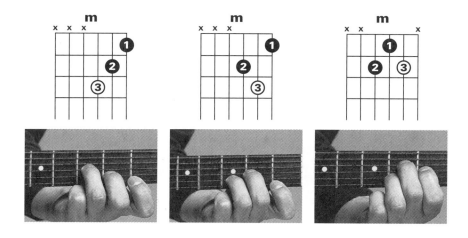

'Texas Blues'

Now let's put these minor triad shapes to good use with this complete 12-bar sequence. Listen to the recording on the CD and then have a go yourself with the backing track.

Above the chord names, we've suggested a rhythm pattern. Don't worry if you're not familiar with rhythm notation - listen to the demonstration on Track 76 and try and pick up the *feel* of the track. Once you've got that just try and play along using the shapes provided.

TRACKS 76+77

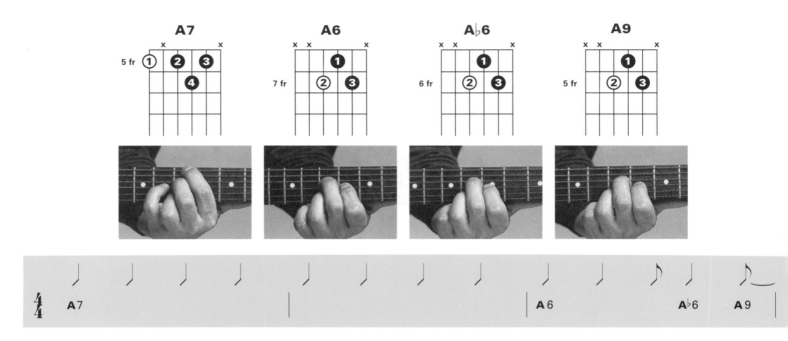

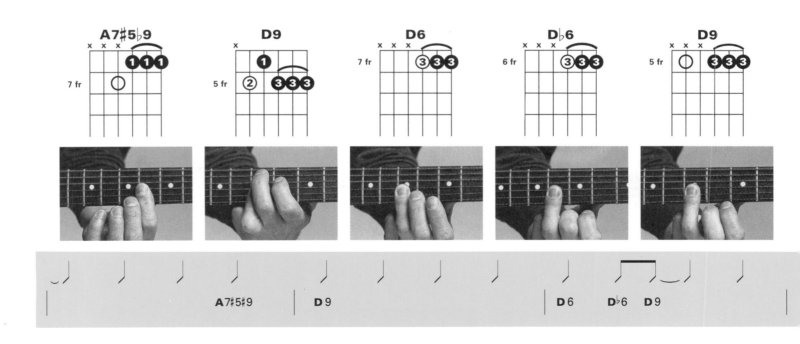

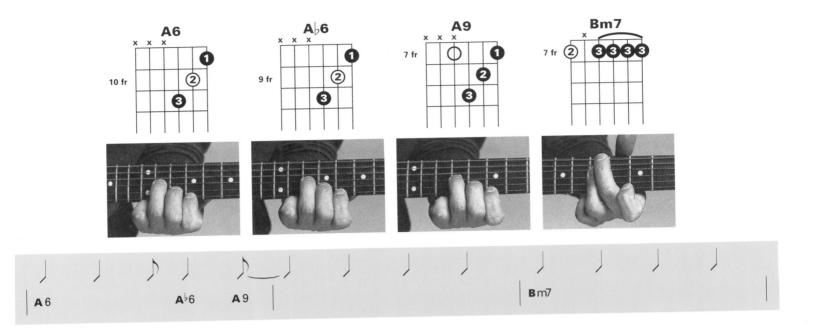

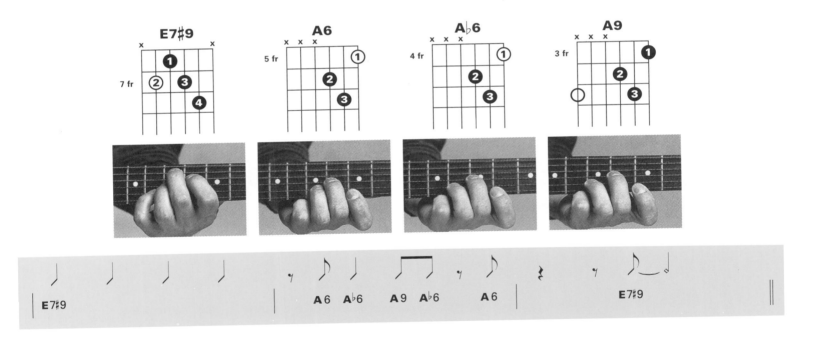

TECHNIQUE TIP
Try sliding from **A6** to
A♭6 each time, without
restriking the lower chord.
Use a clean sound with
the neck pick-up and
roll off the treble to
create a soft jazzy sound.

12. Putting It Into Practice

Chord Summary

Here's a quick sum-up of 12 different **C** chords - one for each type of chord you've learnt. Play each one and listen to the difference between them - you now know how and when to use these chords to spice up a simple chord sequence, so start experimenting!

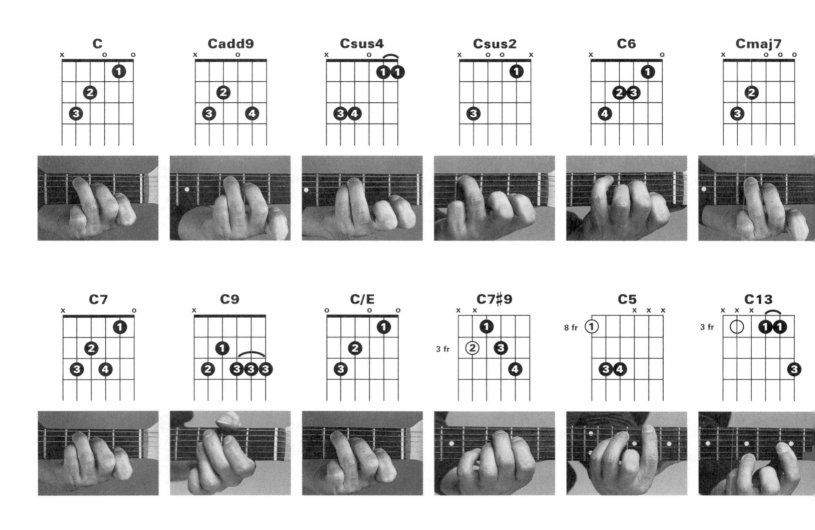

Here are some of the minor chords you've learnt. Check out the subtle difference between **Am** and **Am7**.

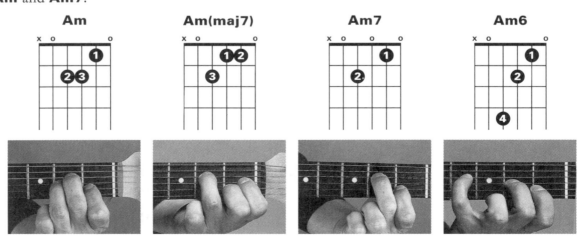

You're now well on the way to becoming a fully fledged Chord Chemist!
To demonstrate the versatility of all the chord shapes and voicings we've discussed, let's take one chord sequence and give it four very different treatments.

The basic chord sequence will use only simple, open chords. Then we'll add some Chord Chemistry to create acoustic, heavy rock, 'Britpop' and funk versions. Each of these will sound very different, but they are all based on the original simple version.

For each version, listen to the example on the CD first, to get an idea of the sound you should be aiming for. Some of the 'treated' versions have slightly more complicated rhythms - it's not essential to follow these rhythms exactly; it's much more important to capture the right *feel*.

'Coda'

Firstly, here's the basic sequence with the most obvious open chords:

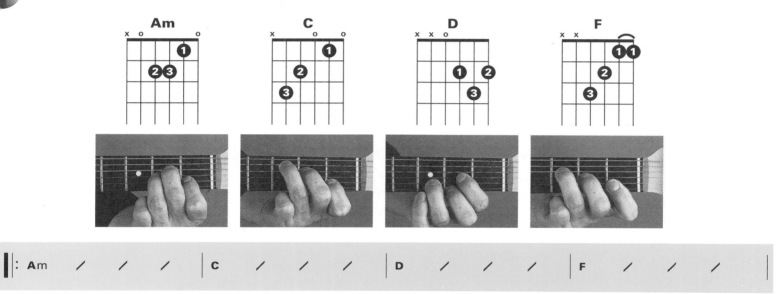

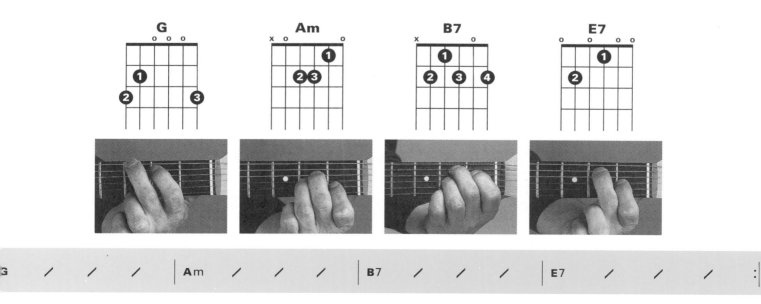

Acoustic

Here's how an acoustic player might approach the sequence - we've added some **add9** and **sus** chords to give this piece more of a warm, mellow flavour.

Once again, don't worry about reproducing the rhythms given below exactly, just strum along and aim for a relaxed feel.

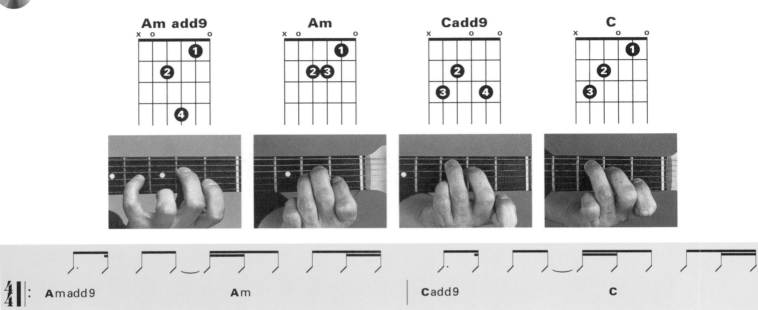

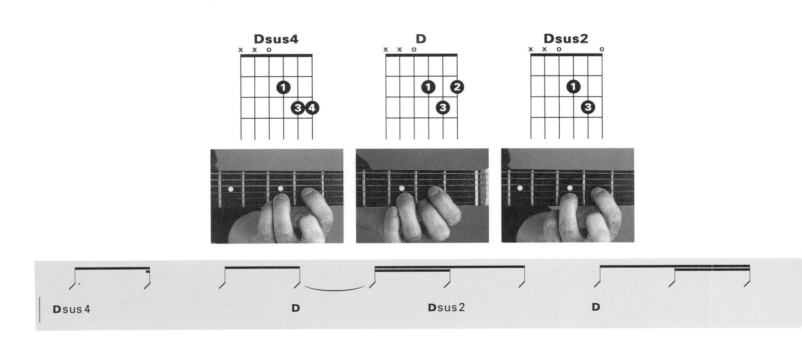

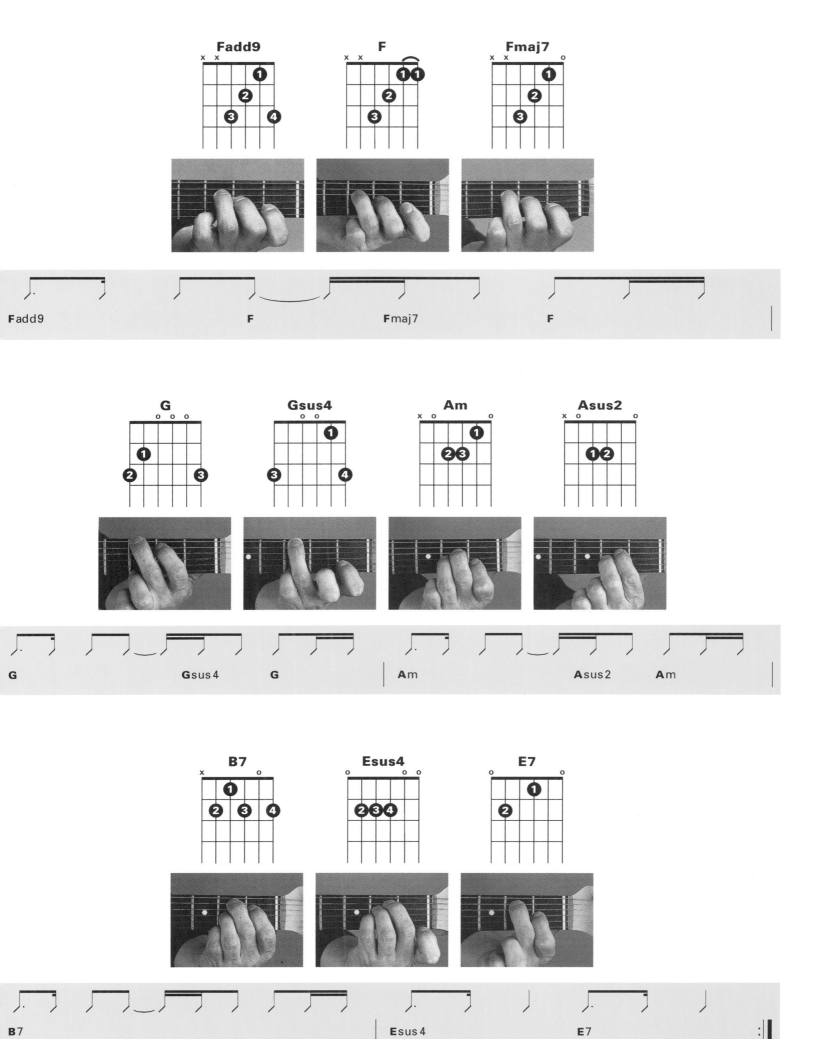

Heavy Rock

A rocker might interpret the sequence like this. Remember - how you play a piece can be just as important as the chords you use. Pick a heavy distortion and mute the chords lightly with your right hand palm to get a 'heavy' rock sound.

Power chords are used throughout, with a Hendrix **7♯9** chord thrown in at the end of the sequence.

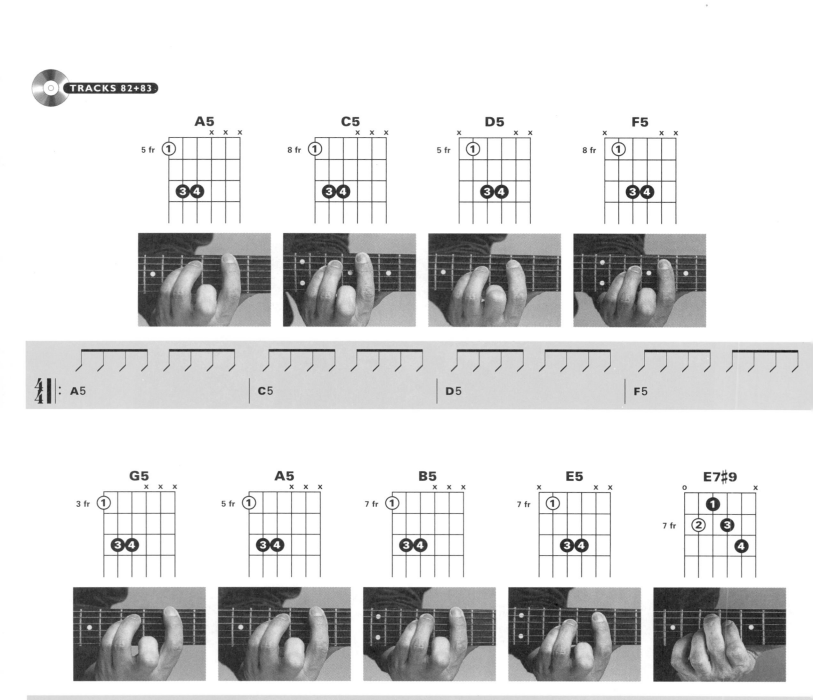

Pop/Rock

Here's a 'Britpop' version - use a warm, distorted sound, and concentrate on the rhythm of your strumming. Notice that here we've used mostly chords played higher up the fretboard - this helps to create that 'pop' sound.

TRACKS 84+85

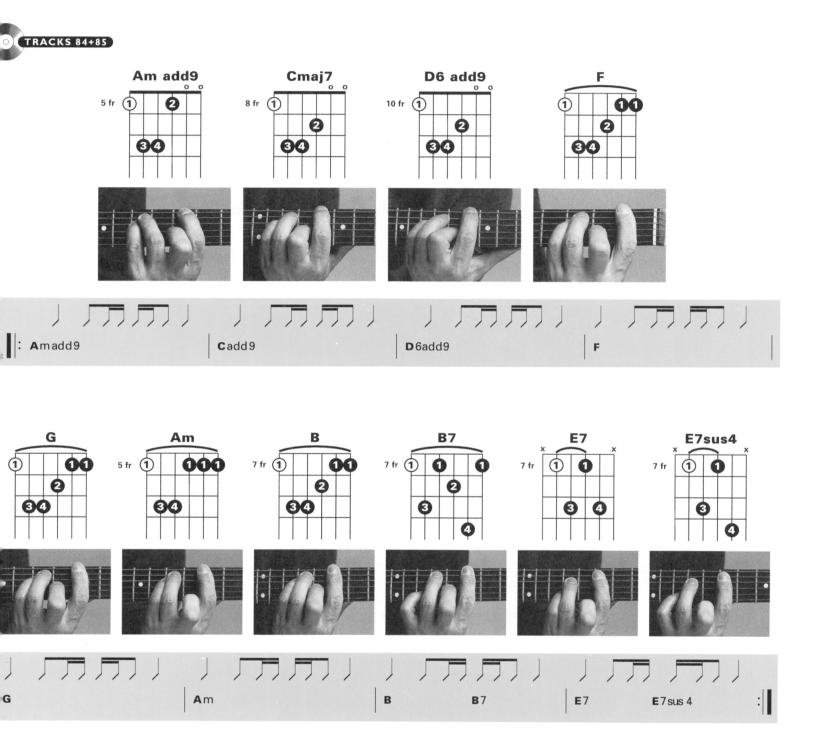

Funk

Finally, here's a 'funky' version using partial voicings, similar to those we discussed in Chapter 11. Use a thin clean trebly sound, and damp the strings with your right hand in between chords to get a really funky sound.

Again, these chords are played higher up the fretboard, so take it slowly at first, making sure you are comfortable with each chord shape. Listen to the version on the CD and try to match the tone quality. Concentrate on the strumming rhythm - and then let loose on your own over the backing track!

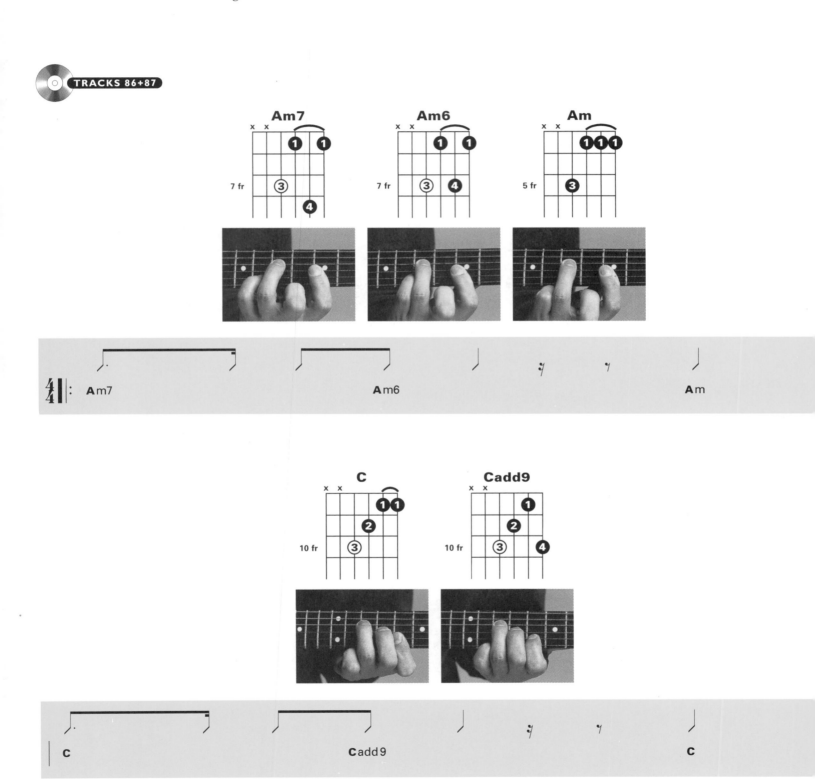

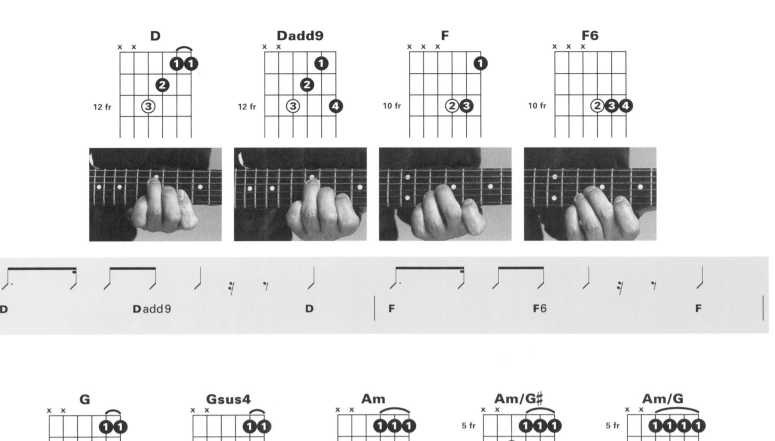

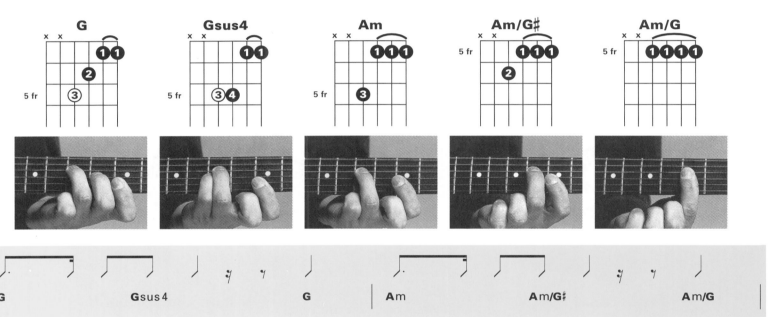

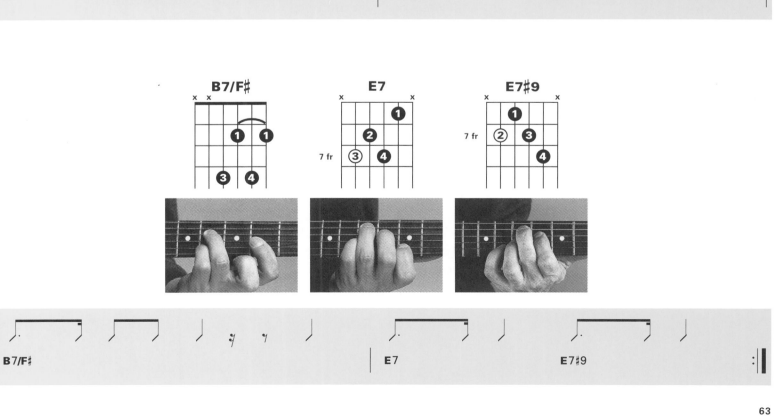

13. The Chemist's Conclusion

Congratulations!

I hope you've enjoyed Chord Chemistry. It's just one of a great range of books designed to help you improve your guitar skills by showing you how to master professional tricks and techniques.

If you'd like to learn more, check out the following books...
or see the full Music Sales Catalogue for our complete list of music books and tutors.

FastForward

The exciting, easy-to-follow system which includes music TAB for all riffs, licks and chords plus handy tips and advice on how to play like the pro's! Each book comes with a CD allowing you to learn and then play along with a backing track.

Blues Guitar
AM951160

Acoustic Guitar Chords
AM950990

Fingerpicking Guitar
AM951159

First Guitar

New to guitar playing? With this series you'll be playing great riffs and solos in no time! Clear instructions and diagrams in standard notation and easy-to-follow guitar tablature.

First Guitar Chords
AM954173

First Guitar Power Chords
AM953238

First Guitar Rhythm Patterns
AM953249

First Guitar Riffs
AM954184

First Guitar Blues Licks
AM953227

Instant Guitar Chords

A comprehensive collection of chords grouped by key, with easy-to-read horizontal diagrams and fingering guides. A portable database of chord diagrams!
AM953414

Guitar Chords... To Go!

All the chords you'll ever need... compact format, easy diagrams and helpful photos... the ultimate reference guide.
AM954240